PAGAN RITUALS

ALSO BY WILLOW POLSON

Witch Crafts

Sabbat Entertaining

The Veil's Edge

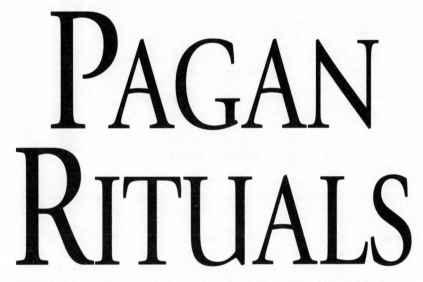

PAGAN RITUALS

SCRIPTS AND INSPIRATION FOR ALL OCCASIONS

WILLOW POLSON

CITADEL PRESS
Kensington Publishing Corp.
www.kensingtonbooks.com

CITADEL PRESS BOOKS
are published by

Kensington Publishing Corp.
850 Third Avenue
New York, NY 10022

All Kensington titles, imprints, and distributed lines are available at special quantity discounts for bulk purchases for sales promotions, premiums, fund-raising, educational, or institutional use. Special book excerpts or customized printings can also be created to fit specific needs. For details, write or phone the office of the Kensington special sales manager: Kensington Publishing Corp., 850 Third Avenue, New York, NY 10022, attn: Special Sales Department; phone 1-800-221-2647.

CITADEL PRESS and the Citadel logo are Reg. U.S. Pat. & TM Off.

First printing: November 2004

10 9 8 7 6 5 4 3 2 1

Printed in the United States of America

Library of Congress Control Number: 2004106178

ISBN 0-8065-2585-1

This book is for our community elders, ritual makers,
and magic workers, and through them,
for the Pagan community at large.

CONTENTS

ACKNOWLEDGMENTS

hanks especially to my Luna Circa sisters and the great folks of South Bay Circles who had the creativity, enthusiasm, and energy to do some absolutely fantastic rituals over the years.

Thanks to my spiritsister Denise Rogers for telling me my rituals rock and giving me the confidence to write this book.

Thanks to Victoria and Bob Johnson, Laurel Olsen, Elderflower Womenspirit Festival, Gaia's Voice, M. Macha NightMare, Starhawk, House of Life, Berkeley NROOGD, Deborah and Buffalo Hamouris, and so many more for your inspira-tions, affirmations, love, and amazing sense of what makes a great ritual. I will always be grateful for what you have given me.

Thanks also to the Great Spirit/Netjeru/Lord and Lady/Spirits of the Land . . . thank you for making me continue on this crazy Rainbow Path even when I was worn out, and for slipping some really great ideas into my head when I wasn't looking.

And I didn't forget my wonderful husband Craig—I love you for about a million reasons, but especially because of your support for me and being there when I need you most. *Elen sila lumenn' omentielvo.*

PREFACE

he book you are holding is a compendium of many things—my experience as a priestess, my experiences as part of the "cast" or "audience" at many other rituals, my love of music, the ideas of other people too numerous to list but given, for the most part, in the acknowledgments . . . in total, this is the book that I so often wished for when planning a ritual but couldn't find. So, like many things in life, I set about making what I couldn't find and what I figured other people were probably looking for, too.

This book was actually supposed to be much bigger, but I had to cut twenty rituals in the interest of time, space, and sanity in the end. It is my sincere hope that I'll be able to do an expanded, revised edition at some point in the future that will include those twenty rituals and perhaps even more as the Wheel turns on and on.

It is assumed that anyone attempting these rituals has at least some basic knowledge in magic,

Witchcraft, Wicca, or some other mystic arts based on the four directions, creating sacred space, and working with deities. Year-and-a-day training is recommended as a minimum prerequisite, and ideally those who will be using this book are experienced at running rituals for other people. All the rituals are worded with the assumption that the person reading the text is the ritual leader.

Why can't you just open the book to a random page and do a ritual with no prior experience? Because it will flop, and flop hard. At the least you will get nothing out of it, and at worst you risk offending the deities and misdirecting the energies you are trying to work with if you don't know what you're doing.

This book was created to be a resource for experienced members of the Pagan community faced with developing a ritual for their own group or in a public forum. Sometimes you've got a fantastic idea that bubbles out of your head and is one of those "I remember when Willow did that great solstice ritual in 1992" sort of things. Sometimes you draw a total blank. The clock is ticking. You stare at the white paper with its little blue lines that seem to mock you, the barren furrows of a mind that has . . . um . . . well anyway, sometimes you need ideas, and that's why I wrote this book. I tried to cover many types of rituals from many cultures and expressing differing viewpoints to give you many things to choose from. You can simply open the book and use each ritual as a word-for-word script, or you can pick out the ideas you like the best and combine them for your own unique event.

Some of these rituals were done by me over the years, or by others in my community, and many were created just for this book and are totally new. Some are serious, some are whimsical, some are in-between, but all are written with practicality in mind. Who walks where, who says what, which props are used, where candles are (and aren't) placed, indoors, outdoors, sunlight, darkness . . . all these elements and more are carefully considered when a ritual is crafted.

All the same, some circumstances may not allow the rituals given here to be done exactly as scripted, so that's where you'll need to adapt. If you are going to give a ritual for a group of people, run a dress rehearsal at least a day in advance to make sure people aren't bumping into each other, and so that everyone knows what he or she will be doing, especially if there are lines to memorize. You'll also be able to spot possible safety prob-

lems, reposition altars so they don't get knocked over, and so on.

Some things to think about when preparing to host a ritual for others are site-specific considerations for your chosen space. If you're outdoors, visit the site beforehand so you know where you'll be setting up things, check out possible problems and make people aware of them, and be sure you have an alternate location in case of bad weather. If you're indoors, it's especially important to know your location inside and out. How do you turn on or off the lights, and how will the various light levels look during the ritual? Is there a kitchen? A place for people to change clothes? A bathroom? If you need to use a curtain, is there one in the hall or will you need to rig one up? Is there adequate parking? You get the idea.

This book also assumes that you, as a ritual leader, will include such basic "housekeeping" in your ritual as giving a five-minute warning before starting, introducing yourself and/or your group if necessary, allowing time for brief announcements, remembering to provide cups for the ritual beverage, and so on. Thus, I have not included these types of things in the ritual scripts because it would be repetitive, perhaps unnecessary, and every group will want to do these sorts of things differently.

Your group and guests may be depending on you to do a good job, but don't let that freak you out—people are far more understanding than you may realize, especially in Pagan groups, which tend to be more relaxed than, say, a corporate meeting or public rally. Delegate responsibilities within your group; even at the last minute if necessary. ("Excuse me, everybody, can I have a volunteer to sort these candles by color. . . ?") Even if something doesn't go the way you intended, simply pass it by and move on—if you don't draw attention to the mistake, you'll be surprised by how few people even noticed that there was one.

They're not at the ritual to put you under a microscope, they're there to enjoy a good ritual and celebrate their faith.

So let's give them some good rituals together . . . or maybe even great ones. Write to me and let me know how it goes. . . . I'd love to hear how you changed something or how people reacted to a ritual element. I may even include your changes in that hoped-for future edition. That's what community is all about!

I

SPRING

The Element of Air

WHEN: Spring

WHERE: Outside

CAST: High Priest/ess (HP/S), four directional priest/esses, designated singer (optional), drummer(s)

MINIMUM NUMBER OF PARTICIPANTS: Five to six

RITUAL DRESS: Robes or dresses in shades of yellow (East), sky blue (South), pink or lavender (West), and white (North). Ribbons and feathers are nice costume accents if desired.

SUGGESTED SONGS: "Air I Am" by Andreas Corbin or "Air Moves Us" by Reclaiming Collective, "All the Air Is Sacred" by Prana, "I Circle Around" (traditional Native American) "Red Admiral Butterfly" by James Galway and the Chieftains

PROPS: Large feather fan, copies of "All the Air Is Sacred" and "I Circle Around" lyrics for everyone, feathers for everyone to take home— either naturally shed found feathers or store-bought yellow ones, little bottles of bubble soap to give out (optional)

ALTAR SETUP: One large main altar in the east of the area with the necessities (athame, incense, etc., as desired), plus feather fan, bell, bubble soap and wand, and a small pine bough

CAKES AND ALE: Mini rice cakes and clear lemon-lime soda

Perform basic housekeeping such as announcements and so on.

If incense will be used for the cleansing, light it now (remember to light charcoal early!). Begin singing "Air I Am" or "Air Moves Us," indicating that everyone is to take up the chant. With the large feather fan, either fan incense over each person in the circle or whisk the fan over each person, brushing away any impurities as you go. You can actually brush the feathers all over them, or simply fan air—either way, concentrate on purifying them as you work.

When you are done, cast the circle as you normally do. Each directional priest/ess now calls the elements:

The East priest/ess holds aloft the feather fan and says:

"Spirits of the East, creatures of air . . . butterflies, birds, bees . . . place of the golden dawn . . . of spring and new beginnings . . . we call to you now, we ask that you be here with us today to aid in our rite. Hail and welcome."

The South priest/ess rings the bell and says:

"Spirits of the South, creatures of fire . . . phoenix, scorpion, rattlesnake . . . place of the midday sun . . . of summer and hard work . . . we call to you now, we ask that you be here with us today to aid in our rite. Hail and welcome."

The West priest/ess blows soap bubbles and says:

"Spirits of the west, creatures of water . . . whale, fish, merfolk . . . place of the setting sun . . . of autumn and fulfillment . . . we call to you now, we ask that you be here with us today to aid in our rite. Hail and welcome."

The North priest/ess holds aloft the pine bough and says:

"Spirits of the north, creatures of earth . . . bear, buffalo, ants and other burrowing creatures . . . place of the midnight sun . . . of winter and rest . . . we call to you now, we ask that you be here with us today to aid in our rite. Hail and welcome."

The Lord and Lady are called to attend the circle as you desire. Alternatively, you may choose to call upon specific Air deities, such as Shu, Mardeq Avalon, and so on.

Now, give the air meditation:

"Please be seated, get comfortable, and look up into the sky for a moment. Take a deep breath, feeling the sacred air fill you, nourishing your body, keeping you alive. Release the air now, feeling it leave your body, taking with it carbon dioxide and other wastes, which in turn feed the trees and plants. Take another deep breath and close your eyes. Concentrate on feeling the air enter and leave you . . . breathing in and out . . . taking and giving . . . the endless circle.

"Now feel yourself becoming lighter . . . and lighter . . . and lighter still until your body is barely touching the earth. Tip your head back and feel your soul yearn for the sky. Your spirit remembers what it was like to fly while you were on the other side. Sometimes you fly in your dreams, and when your body passes away it will fly again. Breathe deeply and remember. . . .

"Feel your body float just above the ground. Feel the air all around you, under you, behind and before you, inside you. Feel the breeze caress you, feel yourself becoming lighter still until the breeze lifts you up, up . . . above the trees, above the circle . . . dance upon the breeze.

"Now you feel your body change, becoming feathered, becoming winged, until you and everyone around you forms a great flock of birds of all colors, all sizes, all kinds . . . the delicate hummingbird and the great eagle . . . the clever raven and the friendly macaw . . . What kind of bird are you? *(pause)*

"We are a nation of birds, spirit birds

remembering how to fly, free from earthly concerns up here . . . we fly. We are free. And we honor the air that takes us here and allows us to be here. We soar and dip, circling and calling to each other on the breezes of the day, the warm thermals that take us up. Then we notice far below that there is an interesting circle formed on the earth, and it looks like a good place to land and rest for a time. But you know that any time you wish to soar again with your bird tribe, the air will bear you up.

"Now take a deep breath, feeling the air inside your lungs again, and transform back to your human form. Gently come down to where you were sitting in the circle of people, and keep breathing deeply, allowing the air to bring you back to your body, within and without. Let it work through your blood to make you more alert, let it feed your limbs so you can move your fingers and toes. Feel the earth underneath yourself once again, soft and welcoming, grounding yourself if you need to by extending some of your energy below you, rooting to the ground a bit or giving the earth extra energy that you may have been gifted by the air. . . . And when you are ready, slowly move your muscles and open your eyes, and be here in the circle again."

If necessary, ask people to refer to their lyric "cheat sheet" for the words to "All the Air Is Sacred" and sing it through once so that everyone's clear on the melody. Tell everyone that the song will be sung to the four directions and ask everyone to stand and face east. The East priest/ess holds up the feather fan while the chant is sung once; then all turn to the South, the South priest/ess rings the bell, and so on, as the elements were called earlier (West = bubbles, North = pine bough). A moment of silence is observed at the end.

Pick up the basket of feathers and walk around the circle to distribute them, saying:

"Please choose a feather to keep and remind you of the power of air. And let us now honor the winged ones . . . our brothers and sisters of the air who inspire us, with whom we can dance and soar. The next song is a traditional Ghost Dance song from the Arapahoe nation. The Ghost Dance rituals date from the late 1800s. The people danced these new songs for protection, to let their spirits transcend mundane reality, and to infuse themselves with magic so that they could become invisible, like the ghosts of their ancestors. This song calls upon Eagle magic to help you soar above things, to see things in a new way."

Sing "I Circle Around" through once so that everyone's got it, then cue the drummers to begin. They should drum slowly at first to get everyone started, then continue a moderate beat throughout most of the circle dance. Speed up if it seems appropriate, but don't let it get too frenzied or people will break the circle. Don't speed up if there are older and/or disabled people present.

Begin a two-step type of dance (right toe, right foot, left toe, left foot, and so on) or a simple bouncy step, clockwise, indicating that all are to join in. Encourage everyone to sing along and dance around the circle, spreading out the circle if there's room so that people aren't crowded together. When the song is over (you'll know when), stop moving and sing ". . . the boundaries of the earth" loudly to indicate that all should stop singing and dancing.

Everyone will need a grounding at this point, so visually or verbally (or both) indicate that they should kneel down and ground themselves as much as needed, taking a deep breath to come back into themselves.

Now say:

"We have done our energy grounding, now I think we can use some physical grounding. Let's enjoy the gifts of the Earth and enjoy each other's company here today."

Play some pleasant music such as "Red Admiral Butterfly" by James Galway and the Chieftains as the directional priest/esses give out the cups, food, and drink. If you choose to give out little bottles of bubble soap, do so during this section. When all have finished their snack and appear ready to continue, say:

"Today we have experienced the magic of the element of Air, both inside us, around us, and through the perspective of the winged ones. Air is the most changeable and whimsical of the elements, and we have explored it in a light and friendly way. Never forget, however, that the hurricane and the tornado can cause much destruction—this is all part of Air's capricious nature. Now that you know this element more closely, think about ways you can work with Air in your own practices at home. Now, however, we must bid farewell to this great teacher and the others who have helped us here today."

Bid farewell to the Lord and Lady in the same manner that they were called. The directional priest/esses now dismiss their elements with their items (pine bough, bubble soap, bell, and feather fan), starting in the North:

"Spirits of the North, creatures of earth, we thank you for helping us here today and watching over our circle. Blessings be upon you always! Go if you must, stay if you will. Hail and farewell!

"Spirits of the West, creatures of water, we thank you for helping us here today and watching over our circle. Blessings be upon you always! Go if you must, stay if you will. Hail and farewell!

"Spirits of the South, creatures of fire, we

thank you for helping us here today and watching over our circle. Blessings be upon you always! Go if you must, stay if you will. Hail and farewell!

"Spirits of the East, creatures of air, we thank you for helping us here today and watching over our circle. Blessings be upon you always! Go if you must, stay if you will. Hail and farewell!"

The circle is opened in the same manner that it was cast. Say, "Merry meet, merry part, and merry meet again" or whatever ending is traditional for your group to indicate that the ritual is over.

Brigid's Triple Blessings

WHEN: Imbolc

WHERE: Outside if possible, indoors is okay if the weather is inclement

CAST: HP/S, three Brigid priestesses

MINIMUM NUMBER OF PARTICIPANTS: Four

RITUAL DRESS: Celtic garb for the HP/S and white linen gowns for the three Brigids, braided hair for the Brigids as well if it's long enough (one or two braids)

SUGGESTED SONGS: "Brigid Song" by Starhawk and Rose May Dance

PROPS: Jeweler's anvil, hammer, sword, large bouquet of mixed herbs in a vase, large box of poetry books, a cauldron, three baskets, containing small bundles of three different dried herbs (such as St. John's Wort, rosemary, and lovage) for everyone; wire cloak broaches for everyone; tied poetry scrolls for everyone

ALTAR SETUP: Three altars set in a triangle in the center of the ritual space, one with the jeweler's anvil, hammer, and sword; one with the herb bouquet; one with the books of poetry in stacks and a cauldron; each has a basket with the giveaway items inside.

CAKES AND ALE: Irish soda bread or short-bread, ale or mead and unfiltered apple cider

Perform basic housekeeping such as announcements and so on. Begin with a grounding visualization:

"Relax and take a deep breath . . . then take another as you let your body relax even further . . . take another deep breath as today disappears . . . as this place disappears into the mists. . . .

"In the mists you begin to smell a hint of salt air in the distance . . . you feel green grasses under you, covered with droplets of dew and water . . . you may hear the trickle of water from a nearby spring . . . and as you take another deep breath, the mists slowly part and you find yourself in Ireland by Brigid's sacred well, tended by centuries of women and their ancestors, and on back into the mists of time. The green grass is broken only by the lichen [like-en] covered stones that dot the landscape here and there, stones that also surround and enclose the sacred well and its clear, fresh, healing waters.

"Hold this image in your mind, smell the fresh, moist air as you bring the spirit of the well back with you . . . bring the spirit of the sacred well and of Brigid back to this place . . . this time . . . this circle . . . and as you take another deep breath, be here now."

Now cast the circle as you normally do, perhaps using salt water as you go around both to draw the circle and to bless the people attending. Call the four elements if desired, or move on to calling the goddess Brigid. The three Brigids should use this invocation to take that aspect of Her into themselves (they may be hidden or with the group as they do this) and prepare for the rest of the ritual.

To soft Celtic music or without music, say:

"Brigid, Lady of the flames, Lady of the spark of inspiration, Lady of healing, you of many names and places . . . we ask that you come to us now, to lend us your knowledge and wisdom, to bless us in your triple aspects . . . *(with more emphasis, arms aloft)* Hear now your ancient prayer, kept alive through the centuries—'Brigid, excellent woman, sudden flame, may the bright fiery sun take us to the lasting kingdom!' *(Pause to feel the spirit of Brigid come into the circle—the three priestesses should move into position behind their altars, back to back in the center of the circle.)* Welcome, Lady. We are honored with your grace and your presence."

The three Brigids nod slightly to acknowledge you, then speak in turn:

"I am Brigid, Lady of Fire, Matron Goddess of smithies, the Bright One, the Shining Arrow. Come to me and learn.

"I am Brigid, Lady of Poetry, Matron Goddess of poets and all those who seek divine inspiration. Come to me and learn.

"I am Brigid, Lady of Healing, Matron Goddess of midwives, herbalists, physicians, and those that need healing. Come to me and learn."

Have everyone stand and, if the crowd is large, divide everyone into groups of three. If a group is short, you make up the balance and go with them to the altars. As each person or group of three reaches an altar, one of the Brigid aspects gives them their gift and says:

FIRE: "Everything is transformed by fire. The hardest things on earth are shaped by it—stone, diamonds, metal . . . even water is turned to steam by fire. Take this metal cloak pin as a reminder of my power to transform. You are blessed."

POETRY: "Poetry is the gift of the spark that lives in our minds and hearts. It is the perfect expression of our souls, a fire fed by divine inspiration. Take this poem as a reminder of my divine spark of inspiration, then go forth and write your own poem. You are blessed."

HEALING: "Without the sun, the herbs cannot grow. Without strength and courage, the healer cannot do surgery or help a woman give birth. Without compassion, we cannot understand the needs of others and help them. Take these herbs as a reminder of my triple healing powers of the sun, strength, and compassion. You are blessed."

When everyone has seen all the Brigids and received their gifts, have them sit down again if they're not already seated. The three priestesses bless the bread and drink as inspiration directs them to, then the HP/S helps them distribute the food to everyone.

When everyone is finished, lead them in the "Brigid Song" chant, which may evolve into a circle dance with the priestesses if desired. Send out the energy to honor Brigid, then have the priestesses stand together with you in the center of the area (or off to one side of the three altars) as you say:

"Brigid, Lady of fire, Brigid, Lady of inspiration, Brigid, Lady of healing, we thank you for your wisdom and your gifts. You of the sacred flame, you of the Celts, you of many names and places, we thank you for coming to us today. Go if you must, but stay if you will. Blessed Be."

The priestesses may leave the middle of the circle, stand to one side, kneel down, or simply bow their heads until the circle is opened. Now dismiss the elements if you called them and open the circle. Say, "Merry meet, merry part, and merry meet again" or whatever ending is traditional for your group to indicate that the ritual is over.

Candle Making

WHEN: Imbolc/Candlemas

WHERE: Indoors

CAST: HP/S plus a helper

MINIMUM NUMBER OF PARTICIPANTS: Two

RITUAL DRESS: Your choice, but short or tight-fitting sleeves are best for safety

SUGGESTED SONGS: "One Small Candle" by Jessica Radcliffe, "Sweeney's Buttermilk" by Mícheál Ó Dhomhnaill and Paddy Glackin, "This Little Light" (traditional) or "Brigid Song" by Reclaiming

PROPS: CD player, candle-making equipment (empty tealight cups, tealight wicks, a double boiler or old pan and coffee can, wax chunks, hot plate or stove, potholders), large heatproof tray or wooden cutting board to hold the cooling candle cups, paper or other cover for the tray/board to protect it from wax spills, song lyrics if needed

ALTAR SETUP: One large altar in the center of the room with the necessities, a statue of Brigid, a large white candle, a large tray for people's items, and a bowl of extra ones (see below)

CAKES AND ALE: Your choice

NOTES: Have participants bring something they can include in the candle, such as a small gemstone, shell, herb leaf, and so on. Also have a bowl of small similar items on hand for those that "didn't get the memo" or forgot theirs.

Start the wax melting and place the wicks inside the candle cups before beginning the ritual. Perform basic housekeeping such as announcements and so on. Have everyone place their special items on the altar before the ritual begins so they can be blessed by Brigid. Have your helper stay in the candle-making area to watch the progress of the wax and to make sure it doesn't catch fire.

Cast the circle and call the elements as desired. Now call to Brigid to attend the rite:

"Brigid, bright Maiden of spring, Light Bringer, Bright One, triple goddess of the Celts, we pray that you come to us now, on your day of honor . . . teach us how to craft our own light . . . teach us how to be strong . . . teach us patience . . . help us celebrate the first of the spring. Bless the things that lie upon the altar with your magic, so that when the good people burn their candles, your graces will come through to them through your holy flame. Hail and welcome, beautiful Lady."

Light the white candle before her statue, then give a brief history of candles and light at this time of year:

"Greetings, and welcome. It's the first day of spring, according to the old reckoning, the day that we celebrate the return of the light after the long, dark winter. This holiday has two common names, Imbolc and Candlemas. Imbolc means "in the belly," and it celebrates both the birthing of the stock animals like lambs and calves as well as the appearance of milk for the people struggling through the sparse winter, storehouses emptying as the dark days linger.

"Candlemas is the day when some Christian sects follow the ancient tradition of making and blessing all the candles to be used in the church for that year. This probably stems from the Irish Catholics, who took the beloved goddess Brigid into their hearts and called her "Saint Brigid." Candlemas is also called "Saint Brigid's Day," and Brigid the Light Bringer is still honored as we make candles to illuminate our rituals on her day.

"So now let us make our candles. Pass by the altar to get your item to put inside the candle, then process to the candle-making area where you'll put your item inside the candle cup and the wax will be poured for you. When you're done, continue on around the circle and back to your seat."

Cue the song "One Small Candle" and go to the candle-making area, or have your helper do the wax pouring instead. Whoever isn't handling the wax keeps tabs on the CD player. When the music has ended and everyone's candle has been made, your helper brings the tray of candles to the main altar and sets it down. You say:

"Behold the potential that we have created! Behold the vehicle for your magic! Behold the vessel of Brigid's flame! Let us now charge these candles with magic, with energy, with potential, with the power of spring's light, with Brigid's sacred fire . . . let us dance the spiral dance and work magic! Everyone, hold hands and follow me!"

Your helper begins playing "Sweeney's Buttermilk" as you lead the spiral dance in toward the central altar containing the candles. At the halfway point in the song (listen to it carefully in advance so you know when this is), you should be at the reversal part in the spiral so that as the song ends, everyone is back out in their original circle and the spiral is done.

Now serve the cakes and ale as people "rest up" from having danced the spiral. Allow five to eight minutes for this, then collect any cups, napkins, etc., and get everyone's attention. As your helper goes around the circle with the tray of candles, you say:

"We have charged these special candles, under the watchful eye of Brigid herself. May your candle bring you blessings and magic as you burn it!"

Have everyone sing along to "This Little Light" or "Brigid Song" as they hold and look at their new candles. Finally, say, "Merry meet, merry part, and merry meet again" or whatever ending is traditional for your group to indicate that the ritual is over.

Imbolc Green Man

WHEN: Imbolc

WHERE: Outside if possible, indoors is okay, too

CAST: HP/S, Green Man, Maiden

MINIMUM NUMBER OF PARTICIPANTS: Three

RITUAL DRESS: Maiden wears a white flowing dress and head wreath of white flowers; Green Man wears green tights and/or a leafy loin cloth and a leafy head wreath

SUGGESTED SONGS: "Jack in the Green" (traditional), "Green Man" by XTC, "The Red Admiral Butterfly" by James Galway and the Chieftains

PROPS: Sweetly scented oil (like lotus, honeysuckle, etc.), CD player, preferably with a remote control, body paints in assorted shades of green, assorted packets of seeds, two baskets

ALTAR SETUP: One large main altar containing a white candle for each direction (can be in a white, clear, or colored holder), bowl of salt, bowl of water, incense, athame, and your other usual accoutrements, fresh greenery and seasonal flowers like paperwhites, snowdrops, hellebores, forsythia, pussy willows, white poinsettias, ivy, etc. (also see Notes below).

CAKES AND ALE: Milk, iced spring water, white cookies, or buttermilk bread

NOTES: Cover the altar with a very long green leafy cloth and make sure it's weighted down securely in the back. Also, make it a comfy place for your Green Man to recline for about twenty to thirty minutes since he will be emerging from underneath the main altar during the ritual. Be *sure* he understands that he cannot pull on the cloth or the contents of the altar will slide down onto his head! Have a slit or flap in the front of the cloth for an easy exit. Make sure he slides or creeps forth slowly—he's awakening from a long sleep. The ideal Green Man for this ritual is young, perhaps an older teen or in his early twenties, and a dancer or actor. The Maiden should be about the same age if possible or younger.

Before the site or hall is opened to visitors, have your Green Man ready and concealed under the large central altar table. The Maiden does not yet wear her floral wreath.

Perform basic housekeeping such as announcements and so on. Give a short grounding for the group, spoken slowly:

"Be seated and be comfortable. We are here today to awaken the spirit of the land, the Green Man, Jack in the Green, the one who is born again each spring with the grass and the grain.

"Close your eyes and take a deep breath . . . and another . . . and now breathe in the fresh breezes of spring . . . the skies are clearing, the snows are melting, new growth is eager to burst forth from seed and egg and belly. . . .

"Now breathe in again and feel yourself forming roots, fresh white roots that reach down into the rich soil below us. Feel yourself reaching up toward the sun, and down into the earth, your essence holding together the earth and the sky as your skin turns green with new growth, just like the Green Man. You are the grain . . . you are the oak . . . you are the flower . . . you rise and grow. *(pause)*

"Now feel your roots begin to come back up into your body . . . and your skin turn flesh color again . . . and breathe in the energy of being alive in this body, in this place. . . . Now you understand a little bit more about what the Green Man is. . . . Feel the roots come back up until the Earth's good energy is inside you, and feel the sun's warmth inside you where they combine and bring you life.

"Breathe deeply one more time and, when you are ready, come back to this place and be here now."

When everyone is ready, you and the Maiden cense and asperge the circle and people using an appropriate chant as everyone joins in. The circle is cast as you normally do—a wooden staff decorated with fresh greenery is a great circle-casting tool for this ritual.

The Maiden lights the East candle and you say:

"Powers of the East, help us to burst forth from the seed and grow into this new season. Hail and welcome."

The South candle is lit and you say:

"Powers of the South, help us to reach up toward the sun and grow strong. Hail, and welcome."

The West candle is lit and you say:

"Spirits of the West, help us learn how to drink up your gifts and prosper. Hail, and welcome."

Finally, the North candle is lit and you say:

"Spirits of the North, help us to reach deeply within and without to be nourished. Hail, and welcome."

Indicate that everyone is to be seated, then turn to the Maiden and ask, "Are you ready?" The Maiden indicates she is ready to receive the spirit of the Maiden. You face each other, the Maiden facing the crowd if the ritual is not in the round. Anoint the Maiden with the sweetly scented oil and say:

"Sweet Maiden, spirit of spring, come now into your priestess. . . . Grace us all with your presence here today . . . help us awaken your partner. . . . You are the white flower, and he is the stem upon which you perch and dance in the rain . . . please come to us now and help us awaken him."

When she is ready, the invoked Maiden silently begins looking around the circle as if she's lost something. She begins to move gracefully here and there, searching people's faces, looking all over, then saddens as she realizes she cannot find the Green Man anywhere. She says:

"I am incomplete without him . . . you know of whom I speak. He is the other half of the dance of life . . . without him, spring cannot exist! Help me call him!"

You and the Maiden sing "Jack in the Green" while the crowd sings along for each chorus, or all can sing it if they know how the song goes. During this song, the Green Man should be invoking that spirit into himself and imagining himself as being both newly born and awakening after a winter's hibernation.

At the end of the last verse, the Maiden turns and faces the altar, saying:

"Awaken, my love! Spring is here and I need you!"

This is the cue for the Green Man to be ready to emerge. The song "Green Man" is begun, and at the first notes of the song, the Maiden steps backward to allow him to come out from under the altar. He slowly creeps out along the ground with his eyes closed or narrow, perhaps on his belly like the short little grasses, and when the music first swells, he should open his eyes wide and lift up his head as if he's taking his first breath. As the Maiden and Green Man begin to dance together, encourage everyone to get up and dance however they like. About halfway through the song you and the Maiden begin using the green body paints on the Green Man and then encourage others to do the same, drawing leaves and vines all over him. When the song is over (about six minutes) all can hoot and yell to release the power, then everyone is encouraged to return to their seats to ground and rest.

You, the Green Man, and the Maiden serve the food and drink to everyone. Play some joyful instrumental music (such as "The Red Admiral Butterfly") quietly in the background for about ten minutes.

When people are done with their refreshments, the Maiden takes the hand of the Green Man and says:

"Thank you, everyone, for helping me to awaken my partner! I'm sure you're all eager for the magic we will make in the months to come. Let us all plant the seeds of hope and joy in our lives!" They get the baskets of seed packets and let people choose what they want, the Maiden and Green Man giving out bits of wisdom as the seeds are taken. They will know what to say.

When everyone has a packet of seeds, the baskets are put away and the Maiden and Green Man embrace, then stand facing each other. You stand behind the pair (rather like a wedding minister) and place your hands on their heads, saying:

"Maiden of flowers and light, we thank you for bringing us your message of hope and for helping us to bring forth the Green Man. Spring cannot be without you. Go now from your priestess and dance in the green fields. Hail, and farewell.

"Green Man, you with many names and faces, we thank you for coming to us and giving us the gifts of renewal and nourishment. Spring cannot be without you. Go now from your priest and become the green fields we eagerly seek. Hail, and farewell."

The Maiden and Green Man then help to dismiss the elements—the Maiden holds the candle, and when "farewell" is said, the Green Man blows or pinches it out.

The elements are dismissed, beginning in the North. Say:

"Powers of the North, thank you for coming to us and giving us your green son so that we may all be fed. Hail, and farewell.

"Powers of the West, thank you for coming to us and quenching our thirst, for without you we cannot live. Hail, and farewell.

"Powers of the South, thank you for coming to us and giving us the power to change the world. Hail, and farewell.

"Powers of the East, thank you for coming to us and helping us to break through to a new season, to turn the Wheel a little more. Hail, and farewell."

The East candle is extinguished and the circle is opened in the same manner that it was cast. Say, "Merry meet, merry part, and merry meet again" or whatever ending is traditional for your group to indicate that the ritual is over. 🦢

The Fertility of Min

WHEN: February

WHERE: Indoors (outside, weather permitting)

CAST: HP and HPS (or two co-HP/S's), belly dance troupe

MINIMUM NUMBER OF PARTICIPANTS: Two plus belly dance troupe

RITUAL DRESS: Green, black, or white

SUGGESTED SONGS: Gentle background music for the love poems, music required for the belly dance troupe

PROPS: Plates and forks for the salad, enough small clay phalluses and green ribbons for everyone to take home

ALTAR SETUP: One large main altar containing a statue or picture of Min covered by a white linen shroud, natron (mixture of fine sea salt and baking soda), pitcher of water and bowl, incense, strips of paper with the names of Min printed on them (use large type, at least eighteen-point, or enlarge the page below and cut out), basket to hold paper strips, essential oil such as lotus or frankincense and myrrh, sheaf of wheat, green salad (see below), small clay phalluses and green ribbons

CAKES AND ALE: Green salad consisting of romaine or cos lettuce, spinach, green onions, pitted kalamata olives, grated carrots, cucumber slices, radishes, and red cabbage. Top with honey vinaigrette. Optional beverage can be beer or cold water.

Perform basic housekeeping such as announcements and so on. Give a brief explanation of the ritual:

"Be seated and be comfortable. We are here today, in the early spring, to celebrate the essence of life, the moment that the sperm meets the egg, the moment the seed germinates, the moment that the divine spark breathes life into the world again. One of the deities that embodies this divine spark of life is the Egyptian god Min, who is also called Amsu [*ahm-soo*] or Menu [*men-oo*] in the ancient tongue.

"You may or may not be familiar with Him. He is usually shown with jet-black skin, the same black of the sacred fertile lands of Kemet by the Nile River. He is also shown with an erect phallus, the obvious symbol of His powers of fertility and fruitfulness. He was originally a sky god associated with thunder, so one of His symbols and manifestations is a lightning bolt. Rain, a rare thing in Egypt, was brought by Min as He fertilized the land.

"Today we will honor Min as the bringer of life. As in ancient times, let us be purified with water and natron so that we may do this sacred work."

Place some natron in the bowl and add some water from the pitcher, saying as you pour:

"We pour water for the Old Ones, for the Netjeru, that you may honor us as we honor you, that you may come to us as we come to you, that you may love us as we love you."

Stir the water to help the natron dissolve, and sprinkle it gently over all the participants. Now encircle the ritual area by sprinkling more natron water. Light the incense, saying as you light it:

"The incense burns, the incense shines. We offer this incense to the Old Ones, the Netjeru, that you may honor us as we honor you, that you may come to us as we come to you, that you may love us as we love you."

Go around the circle again with incense to complete the purification. Get the basket of Min names from the altar and hand it to the person farthest to the east (or, if there's a break in the crowd, hand it to the person farthest to the left). Say:

"Each person is to take a name from the basket and pass the basket on to the person on their left. We will read the names out loud to help invoke Min so that we may honor Him and learn from Him in our ritual today."

You can either take the basket from the person on the end or keep going around the circle until all the names are distributed. Pass the basket around again so that people can drop in their papers when they're done reading the names. The names to be read are (in random order):

Divine essence of life
Bringer of rain
Protector of the eastern desert
Lord of the foreign lands
Lord of the hill countries
Lord of love and war
Fertilizer of the fields
Great bull covering the cows
He who appears with the rains
Lord of the harvest
Bringer of gold and minerals
Guardian of travelers
Tireless lover
Bringer of lightning
Power of creative energy
Opener of the clouds
Father of Himself
Great of love
The god resplendent with his phallus
Lord of eternity
He whose arm is raised in the East
The great inseminator
The god of high plumes
Lord of awe who humbles the proud

When all the names have been read, turn to the statue or image, do the "ka" salute (elbows bent, arms to either side of the body, palms of the hands facing the image), and say:

"Great Min, we welcome you to our sacred space that you may bless us and bless the land below us."

Unveil the statue or image and repeat the salute. Then offer wheat to Min, fan the image with incense, and finally anoint the head and phallus of the image with a drop of oil using your little finger. Any gentle music desired for this section may now be cued. If you are using a HP/HPS pair to run the ritual, have the HPS go first. Turn to the other participants and say:

"Sacred sexuality is part of who and what Min is. Sit back and relax now as you listen to these ancient words of love from centuries ago, listen as they speak across the years to your own heart even now, for love does not know time.

"From the Chester Beatty [bay-tee] Papyrus, Cycle of Seven Stanzas, Stanza Four *(pause)*:

"My heart flutters hastily,
When I think of my love for you;
It lets me not act sensibly,
It leaps from its place,
It lets me not put on a dress,
Nor wrap my scarf around me;
I put no paint upon my eyes,
I'm not even anointed.
'Don't wait, go there,' my heart says to me.

As often as I think of him;
My heart, don't act so stupidly,
Why do you play the fool?
Sit still, the brother comes to you,
And many eyes as well!
Let not the people say of me:
'A woman fallen through love!'
Be steady when you think of him,
My heart do not flutter!"

Now the HP reads:
"From the Chester Beatty Papyrus, written by the scribe Nakht-Sobk [*nak-het so-bek*] *(pause)*:
She casts the noose on me with her hair,
She captures me with her eye;
She curbs me with her necklace,
She brands me with her seal ring.
Why do you argue with your heart?
Go after her, embrace her!
As Amun lives, I come to you,
My cloak over my arm."

Now the HPS reads:
"From the Harris Papyrus, The Third Collection, Beginning of 'The Songs of Delight' *(pause)*:
I belong to you like this plot of ground
That I planted with flowers
And sweet-smelling herbs.
Sweet is its stream,
Dug by your hand,
Refreshing in the north wind.
A lovely place to wander in,

Your hand in my hand.
My body thrives, my heart exults
At our walking together;
Hearing your voice is pomegranate wine,
I live by hearing it.
Each look with which you look at me
Sustains me more than food and drink."

Now the HP reads:
"From the Cairo Vase, ostracon number 1266 *(pause)*:
My sister has come, my heart exults,
My arms spread out to embrace her;
My heart bounds in its place,
Like the red fish in its pond.
Oh night, be mine forever,
Now that my queen has come!"

The HPS says:
"Brother and sister are terms of close endearment in ancient Egyptian writings. Closer than simply wife or husband, it shows the deep affection and kinship the lovers share. Min not only represents fertility of the land, but the flower inside the lover's heart as well."

Turn toward the image of Min and say:
"Oh Min, Amsu, Menu, you of many names, thank you for your gifts to all of humanity! Let us now honor you through dance and celebration!"

This is the cue for the belly dance troupe to enter the center of the ritual area and the cue for their music to begin. Everyone should be encouraged to get up and dance with them in the center of the area, the disabled being allowed to sit in the middle or on the sides as they desire. The free-form dance continues for about five minutes. When the music ends, everyone claps, shouts, does a zagareet (belly dance trill) and so on, directing the energy to the image of Min to honor Him.

The crowd is invited to sit back down as you take your place before the altar. Bless the green salad and any beverages you are serving. Enlist someone's help to pass out cups, plates, and forks to everyone. While these are being passed out, say:

"Lettuce was sacred to the Egyptians, and especially to Min, because it exudes a milky sap when picked that's reminiscent of semen. Onions were another popular food of Egypt and were believed to bestow virility and strength to those who ate them. The other ingredients of this salad were enjoyed then as now.

"As you eat these sacred foods, meditate on Min. Ask Him to come to you, and as you finish, close your eyes to receive His wisdom and gifts. When you are ready, come up to the altar one at a time to honor Him, either with the traditional gesture," (show crowd the "ka" salute again), "by bowing your head, or in your own way. Feel free to anoint Him with oil if you feel moved to do so. If possible, avoid turning your back on Him as you return to your seat."

Stand next to the altar to assist people and to give them their gift of a clay phallus and green ribbon before they return to their seats. Allow enough time for everyone to come up to the altar, and be sure to ask if everyone has had a chance before moving on. When everyone is ready, say:

"The gift you received of a clay phallus was traditionally given to pilgrims who visited Min's shrines throughout the countryside, and we pass this ancient tradition on to you today. The green ribbon is a symbol of growing things, as well as good things. It was common to say "he did green things" in Egypt to denote doing good—to say "he did red things" meant the person was doing evil. So use your green ribbons to do green things as you feel moved to.

"Now it's time to close our ritual in honor of Min." (turn toward image) "Divine essence of life, He who appears with the rains, Great Bull who covers the cows, Tireless Lover, Lord of eternity, your names and gifts are great. Thank you for blessing us today! May you be forever honored and your name never forgotten.

"Old ones, Netjeru, gods and goddesses of ancient Egypt, thank you for watching over us and blessing us today! May you be forever honored around the world for your gifts to us. What is remembered lives."

Say, "Merry meet, and merry part, and merry meet again" or whatever is traditional for your group to indicate that the ritual is over.

Awakening the Earth

WHEN: Spring, sunrise is ideal

WHERE: Outside

CAST: HP/S, four directional priest/esses, string handler

MINIMUM NUMBER OF PARTICIPANTS: Six

RITUAL DRESS: Your choice

SUGGESTED SONGS: "She Changes Everything She Touches" by Reclaiming, "Sing and Rejoice" (traditional, found in the book *Circle of Song*)

PROPS: Various hand-held rattles and shakers, length of natural fiber yarn or string, preferably red, ideally yarn that has been spun by a group member for the occasion, flour for drawing the pentacle

ALTAR SETUP: A small central altar if your group is small, four directional and one main altar if the group is larger

CAKES AND ALE: Egg bread, milk, and soy milk

NOTES: This ritual is especially useful and cathartic if you're having a long, cold spring more reminiscent of winter than the warming months they're supposed to be.

Perform basic housekeeping such as announcements and so on. Give a short grounding and explanation for the group:

"Relax, and breathe deeply. This is the time of change, when the Earth wakes up from winter's slumber. Reach down and feel that energy now . . . something's happening.

"Today we'll be helping the Earth to wake, as we have done since time began. Morris dancers still do this, with bells around their ankles, clapping their sticks together. Other peoples, too, dance on the Earth, encouraging Her to awaken, encouraging the plants to grow, encouraging life to spring forth once again as the Wheel turns. Let us now do this sacred work and keep the circle unbroken."

Have everyone stand and, with the help of your East priest/ess, cense and asperge the circle and people using an appropriate chant such as "She Changes Everything She Touches." The circle is cast as you normally do.

Now the four directional priest/esses call to their elements:

EAST: "Hail to thee, guardians of the East! Spirits of new beginnings and the dawn, come to us, help us awaken the Earth and bring forth the spring! So mote it be."

SOUTH: "Hail to thee, guardians of the South! Spirits of the will and of fire, come to us, help us warm the Earth with your heat and strength! So mote it be."

WEST: "Hail to thee, guardians of the West! Spirits of the ever-changing waters and rains, come to us, help make the flowers bloom and bring the people joy! So mote it be."

NORTH: "Hail to thee, guardians of the North! Spirits of cold and winter, spirits of darkness and renewal, come to us, work your magic so that the time of cold and darkness is past, help the Earth to live again! So mote it be."

As HP/S, you call to Mother Earth and Father Sky, and the spirits of the land:

"Mother Earth below us, Father Sky above us, join in the endless Dance of Spring . . . Sol, kiss your beloved with your warm rays, touch her body, wake her gently, for Spring has come! Your presence here is welcome, and we are blessed for it. Mother Earth, awaken! Bring your blessings to your people. So mote it be.

"Spirits of the land, spirits of this place, awake! Wipe the sleep from your eyes, come forth to bring the land into bloom again. Unfurl the leaves, paint the flowers, bring the dewdrops that glisten like tiny jewels in the morning sun. We are ready for Spring, and we have come to awaken the Earth. So mote it be."

Now ask everyone to be seated and give the meditation:

"Relax, and get comfortable. Take a deep breath and relax further, letting your muscles, your face, your body relax and grow still. *(pause)*

"Like a tree, let your roots go down into the earth. From the base of your spine, your roots go down, down . . . your roots growing deeply into the earth. Down through the soil . . . through the rocks . . . to underground pools of water more ancient than you are. Let your roots drink from this ancient pool and be refreshed. *(pause)*

"Along your roots, more small roots branch outward, searching through the moist, dark soil. Soon, you find other roots . . . roots of the other trees in this grove, roots of herbs and flowers, roots you can't identify . . . Inside all these roots are the Spring waiting to happen . . . the potential . . . the moment of life. . . . *(pause)*

"Touch these other roots and encourage them, love them, whisper that Spring is happening. . . . *(pause)*

"Now travel back up your roots . . . up through your body . . . up and out to the sky. You feel warmer the higher you travel, and you find the sun shining brightly. The sun embraces you gently, feeds you the warmth you need to survive . . . and you carry this warmth and energy back down into your body, into your roots, giving it to the soil, to the other roots you touch. *(pause)*

"Take a deep breath and begin returning to your body, bringing up your roots a bit, keeping some of the energy . . . return to yourself because we have work to do." *(Pause, wait for everyone to get back.)*

Have everyone slowly stand as they are ready, joining hands to form a circle. When everyone is in the circle, the four directional priest/esses, string handler, and you step into the center of the circle. Cue the four priest/esses into their positions (you are Spirit, so take that position now) by saying:

"By the power of Air . . . by the power of Fire . . . by the power of Water . . . by the power of Earth . . . by the power of Spirit, we call to the Great Mother of All! Awaken, and bring us good people the Spring!"

The string handler begins with you and threads the string around each of the five people, then goes around everyone to complete a pentacle. At the same time, all five of you close your eyes, raise up your arms, and use the rattles to raise energy. When the pentacle is complete, give a yell or otherwise signal the other four to stop (agree on this signal in advance). All five direct the energy at the center of the pentacle and down into the earth, then begin to intone a single note together.

The string handler now takes up the powdered chalk and traces the pentacle on the earth as everyone is encouraged to join in the single note. The note should naturally die away by itself (or you can end it by simply not intoning it any longer) and the energy should be directed down and grounded. All five people in the pentacle now walk forward at the same time so that the string falls to the ground on top of the chalk. Leave it however it falls, and lead everyone in the round "Sing and Rejoice," getting people to do it as a round if at all possible.

Now get out the bread and milk for all to nourish themselves and ground fully. Give a libation in the center of the pentacle to the spirits of the land and any other spirits you'd like to include in the blessing.

When everyone has finished eating, the priest/esses begin dismissing their elements:

"Spirits of the North, we thank you for coming to us today and helping with our rite of Spring. We honor you as you honor us. Hail and farewell."

The dismissals are the same for each element (replace North with the appropriate direction). Open the circle, then carefully pick up and bundle the string—you can choose to distribute pieces for people to take home and bury, or your group can burn it, or do other workings with it. Say, "Merry meet, merry part, and merry meet again" or whatever ending is traditional for your group to indicate that the ritual is over. 🌿

II

SUMMER

The Element of Fire

WHEN: Summer

WHERE: Outside

CAST: HP/S, drummer(s), fire performers (jugglers, sleight-of-hand, fire-spitters, etc.)

MINIMUM NUMBER OF PARTICIPANTS: Two

RITUAL DRESS: Reds, oranges, yellows

SUGGESTED SONGS: "Rise with the Fire" by Starhawk, "Fire, Fire, Fire" by Cynthia R. Crossen, or "Fire Flow Free" by Ariana Lighteningstorm

ALTAR SETUP: One main altar with the necessities or, if you have images of the elemental creatures called upon, a small main altar and four smaller altars with images and candles for each direction/spirit

CAKES AND ALE: Your choice

Perform basic housekeeping such as announcements and so on.

Cast the circle as you would usually do, perhaps using a tiki torch rather than an athame or whatever you normally use. Now call to the four directions/elements and the fire creatures that dwell there, beginning in the East and lighting a candle for each one as they are called:

"Great Phoenix, winged one who dies and is reborn like the sun each day, come and lend us your eternal hope. Hail, and welcome!

"Dragon of Flame, fearsome adversary and protector, seeker of knowledge, come and lend us your strength and power. Hail, and welcome!

"Mysterious Salamander, you born of water yet elemental of the fire, come and lend us your protection against the flames that would consume us. Hail, and welcome!

"Scorpion of the Earth, curving danger of the crossroads and of secret, dark places, come and lend us your venomous magic to fight evil. Hail, and welcome!"

Invite everyone to be seated and comfortable, then tell a story:

"Long ago, before recorded history, the people had no fire. In the winter, they would pull their hide robes close around their hairless bodies, praying to whatever powers there might be to help them survive. They huddled close to each other, slept a lot, and simply waited out the long, cold days.

"One day a stranger came to them from out of the East. He was dressed in strange, pale hides, and his hair was golden, like the sun. He asked why the people were so unhappy, and the chieftain said that they were cold . . . so cold . . .

"The stranger asked why they didn't simply build a fire, and the chieftain looked startled and confused, as if he had been asked why the people didn't ride on the clouds or control the running of the rivers. The stranger, seeing their confusion, felt pity for the people and promised to come back with fire to keep them warm. The people said goodbye and stared after the stranger, sure that he was completely crazy.

"Yet they waited for him to return. A day went by, and the golden stranger did not return. Another day went by, and the stranger did not return. But on the morning of the third day, they could see someone coming from the East again . . . someone shining like the sun . . . maybe it *was* the sun . . . some people began to smile, some began to tremble in fear, some simply stood frozen, not knowing whether to run toward him or run away.

"The stranger came to them again but this time revealed his true form to the people as the Bright One, the Lord of Light, bringer of warmth, and fire, and sunlight. He sat with the shamans and taught them how to follow the ways of the sun's path and use fire magic. He sat with the women and taught them how to cook food with fire and tend it properly. He sat with the men and taught them how to hunt with fire so the people would never go hungry and to keep the land renewed with it.

"And so we are the descendants of these first people—the shamans, the providers, the hunters . . . and to this day we honor the sun . . . we work with the fire . . . we understand its power and know how to use it.

"Fire is the great purifier. Fire burns away everything to let renewal happen. Fire keeps us alive, both inside and out. Fire is the passion of lovemaking. Fire is the rage at injustice. Fire dances inside every one of us . . . we are part of it, and it is part of us. When we die, our fires go out and our bodies grow cold.

"Let us now honor that fire inside us, and let us honor the power of fire to change, to transform, to make things happen! Let us raise those fires, stoke them up high, and send the fires of change out into the world!"

Get everyone to stand up and lead them in the chant "Rise with the Fire," encouraging everyone to clap and sing along. Don't use any drums just yet, simply clap and sing the chant, allowing it to build a moderate amount of energy.

When the chant has been going on for a couple of minutes and/or the group seems ready, cue the drummer(s) to begin drumming and drop the chant, encouraging everyone to dance as freely as they want to raise fire energy. Make this a smooth transition so the energy level/flow is not interrupted. When the energy peaks, help direct it as needed, then ground and encourage everyone else to ground the energy as well.

Serve the cakes and ale, letting people relax and recharge. If you were able to get them, bring out the fire entertainer(s) for this portion of the ritual. When the entertainment is over and the food has been eaten, bring the focus back:

> "Fire is our birthright to play with. Fire sustains us in so many ways, especially as Pagans. Can you imagine a ritual without it? Let us honor the fire with one more song."

Lead everyone in either the chant "Fire, Fire, Fire" or "Fire Flow Free." Close the ritual by thanking the spirits:

"Scorpion of the Earth, you of the dark places and secrets, we thank you and bless you for coming to us today. Hail and farewell.

"Salamander of the Water, you of two worlds, we thank you and bless you for coming to us today. Hail and farewell.

"Dragon of the Flame, you who would protect us and challenge us, we thank you and bless you for coming to us today. Hail and farewell.

"Phoenix of the Air, you the ultimate spirit of eternal renewal, we thank you and bless you for coming to us today. Hail and farewell."

Open the circle as it was cast. Say, "Merry meet, merry part, and merry meet again" or whatever ending is traditional for your group to indicate that the ritual is over. ❧

Feng Shui

WHEN: June
WHERE: Outside
CAST: HP/S, eight other priest/esses (one for each *gua*)
MINIMUM NUMBER OF PARTICIPANTS: Nine

RITUAL DRESS: Your choice, something Chinese-inspired might be nice—the ultimate would be robes in the appropriate colors made from Chinese patterned or embroidered fabrics
SUGGESTED SONGS: Soothing background Chinese

"new age" music for the *ba gua* walk, "Happiness Runs" by Donovan (chorus from "Pebble and the Man," found in *Songs for Earthlings*)

PROPS: Nine small colored baskets, each one containing a token to be given as people pass to that *gua:* blue = key; brown = small mirror; green = herb sprig; purple = coin; red = kazoo or bell; pink = goddess symbol; white = small container of clay; gray = god symbol; yellow = small yin/yang symbol. You'll also need a small chime or gong and a CD player for the Chinese music.

ALTAR SETUP: Small tables inside each *gua* (drawn chalk area). Each altar should have a cloth of the appropriate color, plus the colored basket of tokens. The blue altar should also have enough small baskets to give to each participant as they enter so that they have something in which to carry their tokens. (See www.fastfengshui.com/feng_shui_bagua.htm.)

CAKES AND ALE: Rice cakes and iced tea

NOTES: Make sure your ritual area is large enough to accommodate the *ba gua* drawing, as well as room for people on the outside of the drawing to sit comfortably without disturbing it. The *ba gua* drawing should have sections large enough for two people to stand inside them, as well as room for a small altar table, such as a wooden folding TV tray. Make the drawing from flour, and make the *ba gua* prior to when people will be arriving. Orient the octagon so that the blue section faces the entrance of the space, if there is one.

Perform basic housekeeping such as announcements and so on. Call upon the Chinese elements and guardians to create the sacred space, beginning in the East:

"Green dragon of the East, great ruler of the element of Wood, stand with us and make this a holy place. Welcome!"

Move to the South and say:

"Red phoenix of the South, great ruler of the element of Fire, stand with us and make this a holy place. Welcome!"

Move to the West and say:

"White tiger of the West, great ruler of the element of Metal, stand with us and make this a holy place. Welcome!"

Move to the North and say:

"Black tortoise of the North, great ruler of the element of Water, stand with us and make this a holy place. Welcome!"

Carefully move to the center of the *ba gua* and say:

"Yellow dragon of the Center, great ruler of the element of Earth, stand with us and make this a holy place. Welcome!"

Now give a brief explanation of the next section of the ritual:

"Please remain standing. Today we will be exploring the Chinese *ba gua* [*bah gwah*] energy map of *feng shui* [*fung shway*]. *Ba gua* means "eight areas," and as you can see, the octagon before you is divided into eight sections, plus the center where all is in balance. One by one, you will be entering the ba gua here *(HP/S indicates the blue section)*, where you will learn the meaning of each gua. Meditate for a brief time, then when I ring this chime *(HP/S indicates chime or gong)*, move to the next gua. Let us begin now."

All priest/esses should now be in place by their altar tables. The blue priest/ess begins by saying quietly just to the person before him or her:

"You are inside *kan*, that which determines your life path. Kan rules your career, your connections to other people, and how well you interact with them. Meditate now on this part of your life, and how it might be made better."

Allow about one minute for each section, from when the person enters to when their meditation is over, then ring the chime. At this chime, the person is given that *gua*'s token (and, if they are in the blue section, their small basket to contain all the tokens), and the priest/ess indicates that they are to move to their right into the next section. Speaking quietly just to the person before them, the priest/esses say:

BROWN: "You are inside *ken*, that which determines your self-understanding. *Ken* rules your spiritual life, self-awareness, and knowledge. Meditate now on this part of your life, and how it might be made better."

GREEN: "You are inside *jen*, that which determines new beginnings. *Jen* rules your family, your health, and your ability to start things. Meditate now on this part of your life, and how it might be made better."

PURPLE: "You are inside *hsun* [*soon*], that which determines your wealth. *Hsun* rules your ability to receive abundance in your life, and your blessings. Meditate now on this part of your life, and how it might be made better."

RED: "You are inside *li* [*lee*], that which determines your reputation. *Li* rules what you are known for, good or bad. Meditate now on this part of your life, and how it might be made better."

PINK: "You are inside *kun* [*coon*], that which determines your relationships. *Kun* rules the feminine, marriage, and your partnerships in life. Meditate now on this part of your life, and how it might be made better."

WHITE: "You are inside *dui* [*doo-wee*], that which determines your ability to finish things. *Dui* rules your children, your creativity, and the things you make. Meditate now on this part of your life, and how it might be made better."

GRAY: "You are inside *chien* [*chee-ehn*], that which determines your supportive friends. *Chien* rules the masculine, travel, and your benefactors. Meditate now on this part of your life, and how it might be made better."

YELLOW: "You are inside *tai chi* [*tie-chee*], the center and the balance. *Tai chi* affects everything in your life, all the *gua* that you have just been through. Without balance, the system fails. . . . your life falls into disorder. Meditate now on this part of your life, and how it might be made better."

You, being at the yellow altar, ring the chime, give out the yin/yang token, and indicate that the person is to exit back through the blue section and return to his or her seat. When everyone has been through the *ba gua*, the priest/esses leave their stations and you say:

"An important tenet in *feng shui* is that we create the world around us through the *chi*, or energy, we run. Those who look at the glass as half empty draw negative energies to themselves and their surroundings. Conversely, those who look at the glass as half full draw positive energies into their lives. It's a self-fulfilling prophecy.

"Let us now speak out affirmations about ourselves and our lives. Let us all bear witness to the positive energies in everyone here, that they may increase a hundredfold and manifest positive magic in our lives."

Start by speaking out something positive in your life, such as "I'm happy to be at this ritual!"

Then the other priest/esses shout out affirmations as needed to get the group participating. When the affirmations have died down, lead everyone in the song "Happiness Runs."

The rice cakes and tea are brought out for everyone to partake, then when everyone has finished, you should get the group's attention and begin to close down the ritual:

"Great guardian of the Center, yellow dragon of Earth, we honor you as you honor us. Return now to your home. Thank you, and farewell."

Do a small bow to honor this spirit, and bow after each dismissal:

"Great guardian of the North, black tortoise of Water, we honor you as you honor us. Return now to your home. Thank you, and farewell.

"Great guardian of the West, white tiger of Metal, we honor you as you honor us. Return now to your home. Thank you, and farewell.

"Great guardian of the South, red phoenix of Fire, we honor you as you honor us. Return now to your home. Thank you, and farewell.

"Great guardian of the East, green dragon of Wood, we honor you as you honor us. Return now to your home. Thank you, and farewell."

Say, "Merry meet, merry part, and merry meet again" or whatever ending is traditional for your group to indicate that the ritual is over.

Bringing in the May

WHEN: Beltane

WHERE: Outside

CAST: HP/S, May King, May Queen, Summer Army, Winter Army

MINIMUM NUMBER OF PARTICIPANTS: Five

RITUAL DRESS: HP/S should wear a ritual robe of his/her choice; May King and Queen should be in medieval or Renaissance-era attire, preferably in pinks, reds, and greens; the Summer Army should wear summery clothing and the Winter Army should wear wintry clothing

SUGGESTED SONGS: Something lively and Celtic, such as "Boys of the Lough/Miss Monaghan" or "Shandon Bells/Fair Jenny" by Maggie Sansone, "Up and About" by James Galway and the Chieftains, "The Session" or "If I Had Maggie in the Wood" by the Chieftains, "Undrentide" by Mediaeval Baebes, or music of your choice. You might want to try timing out how long the maypole will take and choose your song (or songs) to approximate this time.

PROPS: Maypole with an even number of ribbons, garden hose with spray nozzle, cloth to wrap pole and hose together, wooden swords and sturdy evergreen/oak branches for the armies, flower and greenery garlands for the King and Queen (and possibly scepters as well, can be a single long-stemmed rose, a flowering branch, a formal scepter decorated with ribbons, etc.), games such as cloches (rolling balls at a target to see who gets closest), ring toss, coin toss on a painted wooden board with prizes (good fund-raiser!), limbo, Twister, and other fun summer party games. (The King and Queen can award prizes, so have some little goodies like candles, incense, polished gemstones, inexpensive jewelry or other trinkets, roses, etc., ready to give away if you go this route.)

ALTAR SETUP: Long table along the "back" of the ritual area with two place settings and bouquets of flowers for the King and Queen

CAKES AND ALE: Shortbread or other sweet cakes, wine or cherry juice

NOTES: Prepare the maypole by first winding a garden hose around it in a spiral to the top, then wrapping it in fabric strips to disguise the presence of the hose and secure it to the pole. Be sure to hide the hose under grass or whatever is handy, and connect the hose to a nearby faucet. Next, add the ribbons and stand the pole upright by either digging a deep hole and surrounding the pole with large stones or by sinking a deep pipe in the ground just larger in diameter than the pole. (Test-fit the pole before ritual day!) In addition, the two armies and the royalty will need somewhere "offstage" to be concealed until they enter at their cues.

Perform basic housekeeping such as announcements and so on. Begin with a brief history of the maypole:

"Welcome all, and be seated. You are about to witness and be part of an ancient ritual, one still practiced in many parts of England and Europe in different forms and variations. As you can see by what is before you, we are in part talking about the maypole, but there is more to this holiday than that.

"From ancient times until now, the May King and May Queen have ruled over Beltane and her festivities, the celebration of spring, the onset of summer, and of course fertility of the land and all the Earth's creatures. The maypole can be seen either as the Tree of Life springing up from the Earth or as a phallus fertilizing Her. Perhaps it is both at the same time. . . .

"Beltane, by the old reckoning, is the first day of summer, with the solstice in June being Midsummer Day. Besides the maypole and the King and Queen, other aspects of Beltane include . . ."

The Summer and Winter armies should use the word *summer* in this last section of the history as a cue to be ready to rush into the circle, and should come running in, shouting and fighting with pretend swords and branches, at "other aspects of Beltane include . . ." so as to interrupt you. This fighting goes on for a couple of minutes, with much yelling and bravado, until finally, inevitably, the Winter Army falls. The Summer Army should then shout victoriously and parade deosil around the maypole, finally chanting in unison several times, "We have brought the summer home!"

When the chanting has finished, proclaim:

"Summer is here! Let us welcome their majesties the King and Queen of the May!"

These parts can be pre-assigned or a King and Queen can be pulled from the crowd by surprise (if using crowd members, say the scripted lines on their behalf). If the parts are pre-assigned, the King and Queen can come into the circle from a concealed place or can step forward from within the crowd on this cue. The King and Queen are then adorned with garlands and given their scepters (if using scepters). Prompt them by saying, "Does the royal couple have any proclamations for this aus-picious day?" If the couple has been pulled from the audience, allow them to ad-lib for a brief time; otherwise the King and/or Queen says:

"Thank you for allowing us both to rule the day and to serve you good people this blessed Beltane. Today we celebrate love . . . the inti-mate love two people have for each other, the larger love between you and everyone in your community, the love the gods have for us and we for them, the love between a human and an animal companion, the love between close fam-ily, the love of doing something we truly enjoy . . . let us all reflect on this. Let us under-stand that Beltane is for all the kinds of love in the world. What kind of love do you have in your heart?"

At this point the audience will shout out their answers—if no one wants to start, you and the armies should shout out their answers to get things rolling. When all who wish to have proclaimed their love, the King and/or Queen continues:

"What a blessing love is in our lives! There are so many ways that it enfolds us and nurtures us. Let us now celebrate by working together to weave the maypole ribbons!"

The King and Queen walk to the pole and each pick up a ribbon, then continue:

"All who wish to participate, please stand and take a ribbon."

You do not take a ribbon. When all the ribbons are being held, the King and Queen face each other. Walk around the circle, instructing everyone:

"Everyone should be alternately facing to the right and to the left, forming pairs that face each other—no one should be looking at the back of someone's head! As you walk, alternate between going over and under the ribbon as you pass each person. The people facing deosil, raise up your ribbon, and the people facing widdershins, lower your ribbon. Thus, when the widdershins people pass the deosil people, they will raise their ribbons and the deosil people will lower theirs, and we all go 'over-under-over-under' until we're done. Make sense? Great!"

Cue the music; the dance begins. As the dance nears its end, position yourself next to the faucet of the hose or appoint someone reliable. When the rib-bons reach their end, the King and Queen declare:

"We have kept love alive! We have danced the eternal maypole once again! *(The hose is turned on and they continue.)* May we be blessed!"

Everyone dances in the waters, runs out of them, whatever they please. Music may continue for free dance as long as desired.

When the dancing is over, shout loudly, "All hail the King and Queen of the May!" and all cheer. The royal couple rejoin each other and hold hands. They bless the cherry juice and sweet bread, and place them on their banquet table, saying:

"All who wish the blessings of the Lord and Lady, please come up and share these things with us, for we have wine, cherry juice, and sweetcakes."

You then say:

"Let us now feast in honor of this day! And let us all make merry in celebration of summer!"

The potluck table is opened up for everyone (the King and Queen are first in line) and games are put out for everyone's enjoyment. Allow about fifteen to twenty minutes for people to eat and play, then announce:

"Finish your meals and your games, everyone. We need to close our ritual soon."

Allow another two to three minutes, then indicate that everyone is to stand together in a circle and hold hands. Say:

"Today we have brought the summer in as it has been done since time immemorial. We have celebrated many kinds of love . . . you can feel it right now, through the hands you hold. Give some love to those on either side of you, and take some love in return. We always have a little love to give, and we can always use a little from others, too. Look around you at all the beautiful people here. We are all a bit of the circle, all a bit of the love here today. Take it back home with you and use it well. *(Turn toward King and Queen.)* My Lord, My Lady, thank you for serving and being served today. We could not have celebrated Beltane properly without you. You have our blessings."

They reply:

"And you have ours. Go now and spread love in the world this blessed Beltane day!"

Say, "Merry meet, merry part, and merry meet again" or whatever ending is traditional for your group to indicate that the ritual is over. ❧

Midsummer Bonfire

WHEN: Litha

WHERE: Outside

CAST: HP/S, assisting priest/ess (or HP and HPS)

MINIMUM NUMBER OF PARTICIPANTS: Two

RITUAL DRESS: Your choice, yellows and golds would be good

SUGGESTED SONGS: "Anthem to the Sun" by Rick Hamouris, "Sacrificial Bonfire" by XTC, "Turn Again" by Catherine Madsen

PROPS: Bonfire laid in advance inside a safe area for easy lighting, fire extinguisher and shovel, CD player, lyric sheet for the songs, besom

ALTAR SETUP: One main altar containing the necessaries off to one side, preferably in the south quarter

CAKES AND ALE: Your choice

NOTES: Make sure you have all permits, etc., needed for the bonfire well in advance, and don't skimp on safety and first-aid equipment, especially if there's any wind at all.

Perform basic housekeeping such as announcements and so on.

Slowly and carefully sweep the circle with the besom, perhaps in a widdershins spiral, or otherwise in your favorite manner. When this is completed, you and your partner use incense and saltwater to cense and asperge all present.

Go around a third time and cast the circle with the sword or athame, using your own words or slowly saying, "Three by three we go around, and now the circle is well-bound." Place the tip of the blade downward into the earth to seal and ground the sacred space.

Call the four elements/guardians as desired, or use the following invocations:

"Eastern winds of change, come to us today, help us understand the meaning of the summer solstice. Hail and welcome.

"Southern fires of the sun, come to us today, teach us the hidden meanings of sacrifice. Hail and welcome.

"Western waters of emotion, come to us today, let us learn more about the ebb and flow of life. Hail and welcome.

"Northern earth of stability, come to us today, help us to realize that whatever changes happen, you are always here to ground us. Hail and welcome."

Now give an explanation of the goals and meanings of the ritual:

"It is now Midsummer, the solstice, the time of the sun's greatest power, but it is also the time that the sun begins to die. It is the day that the Oak King battles the Holly King . . . when the Greenman's hair begins to turn brittle with age as the grains start to ripen.

"It's a bittersweet moment for the Lord . . . at the height of his power he begins to relinquish it so that we, his children, may survive another winter. It is the day of the changing of the guard, the day the Lord of the grain willingly sacrifices his own life for ours.

"But this is the way of all things. Life flows and ebbs. Mountains are pushed up and then beaten down into dust. The Lord is born each winter to repeat this very cycle every year. The Lady is maiden, mother, and finally crone. This is the way of all things. Some things must die so that others may live."

Sing or play the song "Anthem to the Sun" as the other priest/ess begins to light the bonfire. When the song is over, hand out quarter-sheets of paper and colorful pens. Then say:

"What makes the plants grow? The sun's energy does. The sun bakes the grasses dry as well, and dries out the firewood. By burning the wood, we reclaim the sun's stored energy . . . this truly is a small piece of the sun here before us.

"On your paper, write down something you wish to sacrifice to the flames. It can be something that you've completed and you want to seal it with fire. It can be something you wish to be rid of forever. It can be a prayer you want to send to the gods on the fire's smoke. It can be something you are willing to give up to gain something else. It can be a vow you make to the old ones. Take your time and think carefully about what you write on that paper, for when it is tossed into the flames, it cannot be taken back. Whenever you are ready, give your sacrifice to the fire."

Now play the song "Sacrificial Bonfire" as all finish writing and toss their papers into the fire. When the song is over, have everyone hold hands in a circle around the fire if there's enough room, otherwise just stand in a circle. Indicate that everyone is to begin slowly processing deosil by saying "now we will turn the wheel of the year once again" or similar wording. Begin to sing "Turn Again" and encourage everyone to join in, even if it's only on the chorus.

When the song is over, continue processing

until the circle comes back to its beginning point, then indicate that everyone is to be seated for cakes and ale. Pass out the food and drink, making an offering to the bonfire when everyone has been served. Use your own heartfelt wording for this.

When everyone has finished eating and is ready to move on, it's time to close the ritual. Begin by saying:

> "Everyone . . . we are blessed by the sun every day, even when he is weakest at the winter solstice. Without the sun's warmth and energy, we would die, just as we could not survive without Mother Earth's fertility. Together, the Lord and Lady give us everything in our lives. We thank them now for their blessings to us, and we pray that we may give back to them in return.

> "And praise be to the North Earth powers, that sustain us and give us stability. Praise be to the powers of the West Waters, teachers of how to let go and the cycles of the tides. Praise be to the South Fires, the spark of the sun and energy to go on. Praise be to the East Winds, shifting and changing, but always around and within us too. We thank you all for your lessons and help here today. Hail and farewell until next time."

Open the circle as desired. You can go back around three times if you wish, or simply open the energy in one pass if it feels like that will work for you. Finally, say, "Merry meet, merry part, and merry meet again" or whatever ending is traditional for your group to indicate that the ritual is over. ❧

Summer Fun

WHEN: Summer Solstice/Midsummer
WHERE: Outdoors
CAST: HP/S, directional priest/esses
MINIMUM NUMBER OF PARTICIPANTS: Five
RITUAL DRESS: HP/S wears white, East wears rainbow colors or yellow, South wears something with flames, West wears blue swimwear, North wears green, preferably with leaves and/or flowers.
SUGGESTED SONGS: "Air Moves Us" by Reclaiming,

"Up and About" by the Chieftains, cheerful harp pieces such as "O'Carolan" or "The Ash Grove," "We Come from the Mountain" (traditional, popularized by Harry Belafonte)

PROPS: Bubble wand with electric fan, a tiki torch, a prepared barbecue pit, wading pool filled with water, bouquet of sunflowers, potted tree (if no trees are to the north of your ritual area)

ALTAR SETUP: Four small altars, one in each direction (wooden TV trays are perfect for this), and a "central" working altar (can be off to one side as well). The East altar should have the bubble wand, bubble soap, and a yellow candle. The South altar should be the prepared barbecue and a lit tiki torch stuck into the ground next to it (use extra lighter fluid since some will evaporate before you can light the charcoal, and make sure your tiki torch can be easily picked up and securely set back down again for safety). The West altar can be in front of or behind the wading pool and should have a blue candle on it. The North altar should feature a large bouquet of sunflowers tied with a ribbon so that it can be picked up and a green candle. The "central" altar should have a gold candle for the God, a silver candle for the Goddess, and the usual tools and embellishments such as an athame, summer flowers, a bowl of summer fruit, sun images, and so on.

CAKES AND ALE: Fresh lemonade, orange slice wheels, sun-shaped cookies

NOTES: Make the event a potluck picnic and particularly encourage everyone to bring barbecue items, which will be grilled on the South altar after the ritual.

After basic housekeeping, cense and asperge the circle and people, using an appropriate chant such as "Air Moves Us." The circle is cast as you normally do.

Beginning in the East, the East priest/ess lights the yellow candle, holds aloft the bubble wand, as (hopefully) bubbles drift throughout the air. S/he says:

"Blessings on thee, spirits of the East, the rising summer sun, the air that floats our dreams to the blue sky on warm breezes. Please come and play with us! Hail, and welcome."

The South priest/ess then lights the tiki torch, and holds it aloft in salute, saying:

"Blessings on thee, spirits of the South, the blazing summer sun, the fires that both give and take life. Please come and feed our souls! Hail, and welcome."

S/he then touches the torch to the prepared barbecue grill to light it. If it doesn't light properly, you should step forward and (carefully!) give the briquettes a little squirt of lighter fluid to get things going.

The West priest/ess lights the blue candle, gets into the wading pool, and says:

"Blessings on thee, spirits of the West, the wild surf of the sea, the cooling waters that bring relief from the heat, the blessed rains that turn the land green. Please come and dance with us! Hail, and welcome."

S/he can scoop up water in his/her hands and let it pour out back into the pool as the words are said. A beach bucket or other container can also be used. If it's an especially hot day, the priest/ess can briefly lie down and get wet, saying the words while dripping with water.

Finally, the North priest/ess lights the green candle and holds aloft the sunflower bouquet, saying:

"Blessings on thee, spirits of the North, the cool caverns and blessed starry night, you whose sun-warmed body nourishes the crops and fruit-laden trees. Please come and nourish us! Hail, and welcome."

Light the silver Goddess candle and say:

"Bright Lady of the summer bounty, please come and be with your children so that we may celebrate the solstice with your blessings. Hail, and welcome."

Light the gold God candle and say:

"Golden Lord of the sun, He who shines upon us all even in this hour of your decline, please come and be with your children so that we may celebrate your life. Hail, and welcome."

Have everyone be seated comfortably with their eyes closed, and then begin the Joy Meditation:

"Feel the warm sun on your face, on your body, all around you. How good it feels! How wonderful it is to be alive today, in this place, at this moment, with these people all around you in the sunlight. Take a deep breath and let it out again . . . and another . . . feeling the peace this perfect day brings.

"This day is also on the knife's edge. The Sun King begins his decline today. He dies now, but He dies willingly, with love for the world, with joy He dances into the darkness knowing that He will become the grain that nourishes us all. This is the joy, the secret treasure of the sun's heart, the joy of knowing that sacrifice is never wasted.

"What have you done for others that brought them happiness? Think now for a moment on this. (pause)

"The happiness you bestowed on others was returned in your own heart. This is one of the great mysteries—energy sent outward is received in turn. Send out joy, and you shall receive joy.

"Joy is also a perception, something you have the power to create in your own life by shifting how you look at things. Some things, like the mew of a kitten, the soft skin of a baby, an unexpected gift, or your favorite food, all bring you joy. But what about the single rose a bedraggled bush has managed to produce despite neglect? Or an ordinary day spent with a family member?

"The rose can be pitied as a sorry attempt by the bush or seen as a rare jewel made rarer by circumstance. If the family member has passed on, what would you give to have one more "ordinary" day with them? Joy can be found through perception. Sometimes living in the moment reveals wonders too easily missed when all thoughts turn to yesterday or tomorrow. Sometimes by shifting where you are, the sun suddenly glints off a gemstone that was missed before.

"Can you think of any ordinary things or events that are really secret jewels in your life? *(pause)*

"Through sacrifice and generosity, joy grows. Through appreciation of the ordinary, joy grows. Breathe in the joy of being alive, the joy of the sun's gift to us, and the joy of being here now. Fill yourself with it and smile. *(pause)*

"When you are ready, open your eyes and see the sun reflected in all the smiling faces here with us today."

When people have opened their eyes and seem to be back, say:

"Even though this is the time when the Sun King begins to die, summer is also the time for good weather, outdoor activities, and the gifts of sweet fruits from the Mother. Enjoy these gifts, enjoy each day as a gift instead of letting future worries or outside influences tarnish the loveliness of the now. What in your life brings you joy? Joy without reservation or qualification? Hold those things tight in your hand before you like the jewels they are, and let them take you through the hard times, the moments of despair, the harsh winter to come. But that cold day is six months off, right? Now is the time to eat good food, dance and sing, laugh and love!"

All priest/esses should stand and motion for the crowd to stand as well, then they should begin dancing to rousing joyous music such as "Up and About" by the Chieftains. Encourage everyone to free-form dance until the song concludes, linking arms, twirling, whooping, and clapping with joy. An impromptu spiral will probably form itself during the dance. If the music concludes and people are still dancing, all priest/esses should stand in place, whooping and clapping loudly to signal people that the energy has been raised and the dance of joy is over. When people begin returning to their places and otherwise indicate they're ready, announce that they should return to their seats for Cakes and Ale.

As people are seated and the servers begin circulating with the lemonade, orange wheels, and cookies, say:

"Enjoy these gifts of the summer sun, a reminder of the joys of the season and also of the seasons to come."

Play an additional piece of music, this one much more subdued but still joyous and reminiscent of summer, such as a cheerful harp piece. After about five minutes, if people seem to be finished with their cakes and ale, have the servers go around to collect any orange rinds, cups, and so on. When they're done, stand and say:

"Nurturing Lady, Lord of wisdom, we thank you for blessing us with your presence today. May we remember your gifts and lessons each day. We bid you hail and farewell."

Then blow or pinch out the silver and gold candles. Indicate that the four priest/esses are to begin saying farewell at their stations. They may use words of their choice, or everyone may use the song "We Come from The Mountain" by Harry Belafonte en masse.

Open the circle and then say, "Merry meet, merry part, and merry meet again" or whatever ending is traditional for your group to indicate that the ritual is over.

III

FALL

The Element of Water

WHEN: Fall

WHERE: Outside

CAST: HP/S

MINIMUM NUMBER OF PARTICIPANTS: One

RITUAL DRESS: Blues, whites, and silvers

SUGGESTED SONGS: "The River Is Flowing," "We All Come from the Goddess," "Lady of the Flowing Waters" by On Wings of Song and Robert Gass

PROPS: Bowl of salt water, sprig of leaves such as willow, cedar, or sage, large watertight cauldron, decorations for around cauldron (white and blue flowers, sand, pale blue round cloth, battery-powered white or blue mini-lights, etc.)

ALTAR SETUP: One central altar containing the necessities with an altarcloth in shades of blues, whites, and silvers

CAKES AND ALE: Cold spring water

NOTES: This ritual can be done inside, but participants won't be able to pour water over themselves, so just have them drink it instead.

Perform basic housekeeping such as announcements and so on.

Instruct everyone to line up outside the entrance to the ritual area, so that they may be purified as they enter. Take up the bowl of salt water and sprig of leaves, then begin to asperge the first person (not in the face!), giving a nod or other indication that they are to enter and be seated.

Cast the circle as you normally would, and call the elements/guardians as desired. Now call to the God and Goddess:

"Lady of the healing waters, Lord of storms, Mari [mah-ree], Tlaloc [tl-ah-lock], Yemaya [yeh-mai-yah], Hapi [hah-pee], Ganga [gan-ja], Poseidon [poh-sai-don] . . . these are but some of your names . . . we know your powers, the powers to nourish, to heal, to bring rain, to wash away, to destroy . . . we call to you and honor you. Please come to us now that we may learn from you, Lord and Lady of the living waters. Hail and welcome."

Now begin the water meditation:

"Please be seated and be comfortable. . . . Today's ritual is focused on Water in all its attributes. If we look at the elements and directions as seasons, then East Air is Spring, South Fire is Summer, West Water is Autumn, and North Earth is Winter. Today, here in autumn, we come to the harvest . . . the wrapping up of loose ends toward completion . . . the beginning of contemplation. We move from youth to maturity . . . we see the sun beginning to set in preparation for night. It is the twilight time.

"Close your eyes now and take a deep breath. Feel the air enter and leave your lungs, almost like the tide that flows and ebbs on the seashore. You begin to catch a scent of salt water . . . you taste the spicy moisture on your tongue as you picture yourself on the beach. You walk toward the sea, and it is a beautiful, colorful, glorious sunset. Long shadows cast themselves around you as your toes find the firm, wet sand at the edge of the water. Take a few more steps, then stand for a moment and watch the waves move in and out . . . letting the ocean play around your feet and ankles. *(pause)*

"Watch the waves as they move . . . notice how they have a rhythm that makes them so soothing to watch . . . so healing . . . you sit down at the water's edge and feel the edge of the ocean around you, gently washing over you . . . sea fingers caressing your body and then taking themselves back to the sea again . . . feel the water giving you energy, washing you clean, then taking away the things you don't

want any longer. Feel it giving . . . washing . . . taking . . . giving . . . washing . . . taking . . . *(pause)*

"See the cycle of each wave. Being born, cresting, washing ashore to rest, and back to the source again. Water is like that. The clouds come from evaporation, then rain down upon us, then become rivers, and eventually return to the sea. We can see ourselves in a cycle like that too . . . being born . . . becoming the crashing wave, resting and letting go, and returning to the source to begin again.

"We can also see ourselves as the newborn clouds, then the storm, then the river which returns to the sea. Perhaps you see your life as a little boat on that river, making its way down through the rapids to the calm delta and eventually out into the sea. But all the ends are the same—the ocean. *(pause)*

"Feel the water on your body as you stand up again, letting the foamy tide surround your ankles. It's time to come back to our ritual space, so you walk slowly back up the beach . . . the firm, wet sand changing to dry and soft under your feet. As you walk back, you take a few deep breaths, and . . . finally . . . step up onto the dunes where the rest of our ritual waits. And, as you are ready, open your eyes and be here now."

As people are coming back, get out the cold water and cups. When all are ready, say:

"We have water here for you to experience, whether you'd like to drink it, pour it out in libation, pour it over yourself in healing or blessing. . . . We also have a cauldron in the center of the circle for libations, so please pour some of your water into the cauldron. We're going to be singing "The River Is Flowing" as we work with our water."

You or a designated singer gets everyone started singing and keeps the song going as all do as they like with their water. When everyone has finished, have all join hands and change the chant to "We All Come from the Goddess." Very slowly begin leading everyone in a slow spiral dance into and out from the cauldron of water. Don't let it get rowdy—It should be a slow meditation.

When the spiral is done, let the chant fade away and say, "Now ground yourself" or else simply lead by example. Give everyone a moment to ground, then say:

"Sacred waters of life, we thank you for your lessons today, and for everything you give to us. May we give back to you what we can by not wasting you and not polluting you.

"Lady and Lord of the waters in all your forms, in all your names, from all your peoples, we thank you for your blessings . . . we thank you for being here today to teach us and heal us. Blessings to you always."

Dismiss the elements/guardians as they were called, and open the circle in your usual manner. Say, "Merry meet, merry part, and merry meet again" or whatever ending is traditional for your group to indicate that the ritual is over.

Egyptian New Year

WHEN: August (check an online calendar for the exact date)

WHERE: Outside if possible, indoors is okay, too

CAST: HP/S, belly dance troupe

MINIMUM NUMBER OF PARTICIPANTS: One plus dance troupe

RITUAL DRESS: Something evocative of ancient

Egypt, such as a white sheer linen or cotton gown, gaballah robe, wrap skirt, and so on.

SUGGESTED SONGS: Joyous and lively Egyptian music for the dancers

PROPS: The four canopic jars representing Duamatef, Hapi, Qebsenef, and Imsety, as well as statues of the goddesses Isis, Nepthys, Neith, and Selket. A reproduction Egyptian wand is a great tool if you can find or make one (it looks like a curved boomerang decorated with deities; pictures are available online or in books), or you can use your regular circle casting tool(s).

ALTAR SETUP: One main altar large enough for plates of offering foods (direct your guests to place their potluck dishes here) featuring a statue of Osiris with a green candle, incense, flowers and greenery, plus a smaller altar in each quarter. Set up your quarter altars thus: East is Duamatef (jackal) and Neith; South is Imsety (human) and Isis; West is Qebsenef (falcon) and Selket, North is Hapi (baboon) and Nepthys; candles can be colored or white, your choice, and each direction should also be honored with incense

CAKES AND ALE: Beer, water, and herbed honey cakes

NOTES: The bigger the dance troupe the better! And audience participation is strongly encouraged—ask the dancers to have people get up with them if they can be convinced (but not strong-armed).

Perform basic housekeeping such as announcements and so on. Begin the ritual by saying:

"Today we celebrate the ancient Egyptian New Year, which began with the rising of the star Sirius above the horizon and the annual flooding of the Nile in ancient times. Since the completion of the Aswan dam, the Nile no longer floods, so we now rely on Sirius alone to be our guide. Let us begin by creating sacred space to honor the Netjeru [*net-cher-oo*], the Egyptian name for that assembly of gods and goddesses."

To cast the circle, you can either do it as you normally would or use the Egyptian wand. If you use the wand, touch it to the ground and draw a circle in the dirt or on the floor around your ritual area with it. Then say:

"Let the quarters be called, beginning in the East where the sun is born each day from the belly of Nut [*newt*] the goddess of the sky."

You or the designated priest/esses call the quarters, beginning in the East:

"Duamatef [*doo-ah-mah-teff*], lord and guardian of the East, Neith [*neeth*], lady and guardian of the East, come now and lend your aid to our sacred rite, protect this circle and all within it. *Iwi imahw."* [*ee-wee im-ah-hew*, means "welcome revered ones"]

Light the candle for that direction and move on to the South:

"Imsety [*im-set-ee*], lord and guardian of the South, Isis [*eye-sis*], lady and guardian of the South, come now and lend your aid to our sacred rite, protect this circle and all within it. *Iwi imahw."*

Light the candle for that direction and move on to the West:

"Qebsenef [*keb-sen-eff*], lord and guardian of the West, Selket [*sel-ket*], lady and guardian of the West, come now and lend your aid to our sacred rite, protect this circle and all within it. *Iwi imahw."*

Light the candle for that direction and move on to the North:

"Hapi [*hah-pee*], lord and guardian of the North, Nepthys [*nep-this*], lady and guardian of the North, come now and lend your aid to our sacred rite, protect this circle and all within it. *Iwi imahw."*

After the North candle is lit, say:

"Be comfortable, for now I have a story to tell. It is one of sorrow and joy, treachery and loyalty, death and rebirth. *(HP/S lights the green candle in front of Osiris.)* Lord Osiris, Ausar [*ow-sar*] as you are known in your native land, we honor you today as well. For it is your story that I tell, of how you came to be the king of life and death. *(HP/S turns back to audience.)*

"Osiris, Isis, and Set were all children of Nut [*newt*], the sky goddess, and Geb, the god of the earth. Osiris, being the firstborn, reigned as king over Egypt and his sister Isis was his wife and queen. Set, the god of chaos and raw power was intensely jealous of Osiris, and schemed to put an end to him so that he, Set, could have the throne.

"On Osiris' birthday, Set threw his brother a party. Among the day's festivities was a contest—whoever could fit into an exquisite golden coffin would get to take it home as a prize. Everyone at the party took turns getting into the coffin, but of course only Osiris fit inside it perfectly. Set and his accomplices slammed the lid closed, sealed it tightly, and threw it into the Nile. By the time Isis discovered what had happened, the golden coffin was lost in the river.

"Isis wept, and mourned, and tore at her hair and clothes, searching for her beloved husband

Osiris in the Nile, but she was unable to find him. She wandered through all of Egypt and beyond, searching for what seemed an eternity. Then one day, she heard some girls near the river talking about a golden coffin that they had seen floating down the Nile. Disguising herself as a hairdresser, she talked with the girls, braiding their hair and smoothing it with fragrant glistening oils. Thrilled with their new hairdos, the girls showed Isis where the coffin that encased her husband lay. She opened it, and Osiris lay within—he was dead, but looked as if he were only sleeping.

"Isis was bringing the coffin home again when Set met her and seized the body of her husband, tearing it into pieces and flinging them far and wide across Egypt. Isis knew she would need help this time and asked her sister Nepthys [*nep-this*] to help look for the pieces. Whenever they found one, they kept it and then erected a temple to Osiris on the spot, thus keeping his memory alive and confusing Set as to where Osiris might be at the same time.

"Eventually the sisters found all the pieces except one—his phallus. A magic one was created and attached to his body, then Isis used her wings to fan the breath of life back into her husband. Their child Horus, the falcon-headed god, was then conceived, and Isis was over-joyed—not only had she gotten her husband back, but she was now expecting a child!

"Her joy turned to sadness, however, as Osiris explained that he had been doing much in the Underworld during his existence there. He had brought order to the chaos, and set up ways that people could safely navigate the treacherous path to everlasting life. He was now king of the Underworld and protector of the dead on their way to heaven, an important duty that could not be abandoned. Isis understood that he had to go back. At least now she knew where to find her husband.

"But who would rule the earthly throne? Surely not Set, Isis mused as the child inside her grew . . . but the story of Set and Horus is best left for another time, as it encompasses eighty years.

"The New Year's celebration that we are enjoying today is heralded by the rising of the star Sirius over the horizon, known to the Egyptians as the goddess Sopdet [*sop-det*]. Her appearance meant that the Nile would soon flood and bring the black silt that nourished the crops. Osiris represents that life force, which is why he is usually depicted with green skin to match the plants he causes to rise. As the Nile floods, and Osiris brings life to the land, the people flourish for another year.

"Now let us rejoice and be nourished! Here

are honey cakes and a drink to quench your thirst. And as we share the blessings and bounty of Osiris together, let us also enjoy the ancient entertainment of festival dancers!"

This is the cue for the belly dance troupe, who should now move into the center of the area or, if you are in a hall with a stage, should move onto the stage. Ask the audience for a few helpers to distribute the beverages and cakes. The food and dance portion should run for about ten minutes, then at the end of a song, raise your arms and say:

"Thank you (name of troupe)! And thank you, Netjeru! May you love us as we love you! Let us all now think upon the negative confession. It is called "negative" because it says things the person has not done in order to live a good life. Scholars believe that the biblical Ten Commandments is descended from this declaration, which is included in the Book of the Dead, the spells and utterances of those passing through the Underworld. Close your eyes, and as you listen to me read the negative confession, think on each thing. . . . Would you be able to pass the test? . . . (*Pause briefly between each.*)

"One. I have not treated others unfairly.
 Two. I have not robbed anyone.
 Three. I have not done violence to anyone.

Four. I have not committed theft.
Five. I have not committed murder.
Six. I have not cheated anyone.
Seven. I have not acted deceitfully.
Eight. I have not stolen the things that belong to the Netjeru.
Nine. I have not told lies.
Ten. I have not been neglectful of my responsibilities.
Eleven. I have not uttered evil words.
Twelve. I have not deprived another of food.
Thirteen. I have not committed fraud.
Fourteen. I have not lost my temper and become angry.
Fifteen. I have invaded no one's land.
Sixteen. I have not slaughtered animals that belong to the Netjeru.
Seventeen. I have not ruined ploughed lands.
Eighteen. I have not been an eavesdropper.
Nineteen. I have not set my lips in motion against anyone.
Twenty. I have not been angry without due cause.
Twenty-one. I have not committed adultery.
Twenty-two. I have not betrayed my own standards.
Twenty-three. I have not betrayed my lover.
Twenty-four. I have not caused anyone to be afraid.

Twenty-five. I have not uttered fiery words.

Twenty-six. I have not ignored the words of right and truth.

Twenty-seven. I have not caused anyone to weep.

Twenty-eight. I have not uttered blasphemies.

Twenty-nine. I have not acted with revenge.

Thirty. I have not been impatient.

Thirty-one. I have not violated the sacredness of my body.

Thirty-two. I have not multiplied my speech overmuch.

Thirty-three. I have not condoned or done evil.

Thirty-four. I have not worked treason.

Thirty-five. I have not polluted running water.

Thirty-six. I have not bragged or been arrogant.

Thirty-seven. I have not uttered curses against the Netjeru or thought scornfully about them.

Thirty-eight. I have not been insolent.

Thirty-nine. I have not practiced favoritism.

Forty. I have not become rich by unethical means.

Forty-one. I have not uttered curses against that which belongs to the Netjeru.

Forty-two. I have not been desirous of more than my rightful share.

"When you are ready, you may open your eyes. How did everyone do? *(Pause for inevitable laughter.)* As you can see, a code for how to be a good person is a very ancient thing, important enough to the Egyptians that they provided their dead with a 42-item checklist upon their departure.

"And speaking of departing, this ritual has just about come to an end. Thank you all for being here to celebrate the Egyptian New Year and honor Osiris, king of life and death. Let us now say farewell to the gods and goddesses who have helped to watch over us during our ritual."

If they wish to participate, the belly dance troupe may come back out and ring zils after each *"Hotep sedja"* is said. The elements are dismissed, beginning in the North. Begin by saying:

"Hapi [*hah-pee*], lord and guardian of the North, Nepthys [*nep-this*], lady and guardian of the North, we thank you for your presence here today. May you feast with us now and be forever honored. *Hotep sedja* [*ho-tep sedge-ah*, means "be satisfied/at peace and depart"].

"Qebsenef [*keb-sen-eff*], lord and guardian of the West, Selket [*sel-ket*], lady and guardian of the West, we thank you for your presence here today. May you feast with us now and be forever honored. *Hotep sedja*.

"Imsety [*im-set-ee*], lord and guardian of the South, Isis [*eye-sis*], lady and guardian of the

South, we thank you for your presence here today. May you feast with us now and be forever honored. *Hotep sedja.*

"Duamatef [*doo-ah-mah-teff*], lord and guardian of the East, Neith [*neeth*], lady and guardian of the East, we thank you for your presence here today. May you feast with us now and be forever honored. *Hotep sedja.*"

The East candle is extinguished and the circle is opened in the same manner that it was cast. Say, "May the blessings of the Netjeru be with you always!" or whatever ending is traditional for your group to indicate that the ritual is over. Now have your sacred feast with the foods from the main altar, blessed by the Netjeru themselves. 🍃

Grains of the Earth

WHEN: September

WHERE: Outside

CAST: HP/S, four grain priest/esses

MINIMUM NUMBER OF PARTICIPANTS: Five

RITUAL DRESS: HP/S wears something harvesty, East wears yellow, South wears black, West wears red, North wears white

SUGGESTED SONGS: "Air I Am" by Andreas Corbin or "Air Moves Us" by Reclaiming, "All Among the Barley" (traditional), "No End to the Circle" by Starhawk

PROPS: One Asian ceramic bowl containing rice, one gourd bowl containing wheat, one bowl-shaped basket containing corn, one plain stoneware bowl containing oats, six- to twelve-inch corn woman made of husks, a straw man the same size as the corn woman, a well-laid fire pit (or outdoor fireplace, or even a barbecue) in the center of the circle.

ALTAR SETUP: One small main altar with the necessary tools plus the corn woman and straw man, four directional altars: East has a yellow candle and the bowl of rice, South has a black candle and the gourd of wheat, West has a red candle and the basket of corn, North has a white candle and the bowl of oats

CAKES AND ALE: Beverage of your choice and four kinds of breads (for example, mini rice cakes, wheat crackers, mini corn muffins, and mini oat cakes)

NOTES: If you are lucky enough to have a diverse group of participants to draw from, it would be ideal to have the East person be Asian, the South person be African-American or Arabic, the West person be Native American, and the North person be Caucasian.

Perform basic housekeeping such as announcements and so on. Cense and asperge the circle of participants to a chant of your choice, such as "Air I Am" or "Air Moves Us." Next, cast the circle, saying:

> "As I encircle this sacred place, let us encircle the earth and learn from Her people. May this ground be holy ground. Nourish our minds, nourish our bodies, nourish our souls. We are one."

Light the fire in the center, saying:

> "I light this sacred fire that we may come together, people of all nations, people of the four directions, that we may come together as one in this place. So mote it be." (or "Ho," or

"Blessed Be," or "Amen," or whatever you wish to end with here)

Introduce the four grains of the four directions by saying:

> "This is the time of the harvest, when people bring in the crops and the grains. All over the world, people are grinding the grains to make bread, or cooking them to make soup, or saving them for the long winter ahead. All over the world, people are celebrating the gift of grain, as we do here today. To the East, to the South, to the West, to the North, let us honor the grain spirits and their gifts to us. Come now, spirits, and teach us!"

At this cue, the four grain priest/esses enter, one by one, saying as they each take their places at their altars:

> EAST: "I am the rice spirit of the East, the place of the sunrise. I am the pale green shoots that come up from the pools where the fish spawn. I feed my people, and I feed the world."
>
> SOUTH: "I am the wheat spirit of the South, the place of the midday sun. I am the strong green grasses that grow tall on the edge of the desert. I feed my people, and I feed the world."
>
> WEST: "I am the corn spirit of the West, the place of the setting sun. I am the ripened kernels that emerge from the stalks under the crimson sky. I feed my people, and I feed the world."

NORTH: "I am the oat spirit of the North, the place of night. I am the harvested seeds in the storehouse, the child of the dead grasses. I feed my people, and I feed the world."

Now say:

"We thank you for your presence! You honor us by being here today to teach us about your gifts. Now we will honor you by saying how grain has blessed our lives. *(Turn to audience.)* We have all eaten bread, or cold cereal, or morning hot cereal, or corn on the cob, or rice pudding, or fortune cookies, or any one of perhaps millions of things made with grain. How has grain enriched your life? Speak out and let the spirits know!"

You can go first if people seem reluctant to start. When everyone has said what they want to say, finish with:

"Isn't it surprising how such a simple thing makes the world go around. The seeds of grasses feeding us all in so many ways, the good memories. . . . We should remember where this food comes from and honor that every day.

"Now let us sing the praises of more kinds of grain with a traditional English song called "All Among the Barley." If you know it, sing along, and if you don't, try to join in on the chorus, which should be easy to pick up."

Sing the chorus once or twice (or have a designated singer help with this), then lead everyone in the song. Applause for everyone is encouraged! Next, move the focus back to the four grain spirits by saying:

"The grains of the world are diverse indeed! Now let us hear the wisdom of these that have come into our circle today."

EAST: "I am rice, gift of the gods, one of the most precious things to the Asian people above pearls and jade. Since the dawn of time I have been grown in China, Japan, India, Vietnam, and other lands of that region. I am given to the poor, that they may live. I am eaten by the rich, who make delicacies of me. My traditions are many, and my forms are many. Blessings to you now and always."

(After speaking, each priest/ess pours a little grain from his or her basket into the fire.)

SOUTH: "I am wheat, the child of wild grasses from Mesopotamia and Egypt. I have been found in the tombs of the pharaohs, and bread made from me fed everyone from pyramid laberors to the gods themselves in daily offering. In Rome, the poor were given loaves of wheat bread so they would not starve. Later in England, and later still in America, wheat sustains nations. My traditions are many, and my forms are many. Blessings to you now and always."

WEST: "I am corn, the rainbow spirit of the Americas. I sustained the native peoples for thousands of years and still take part in their ceremonies today. My pollen blesses girls and turns them into women. My ground meal is sprinkled in offerings. I am made into bread, eaten whole, or even turned into sweet syrup for making candy. My traditions are many, and my forms are many. Blessings to you now and always."

NORTH: "I am oat, the dancer on the wind. Europeans first cultivated me about two thousand years ago, and cakes made from me have long been used in offering to the gods. I have fed both animals and humans for many centuries, especially in Scotland, and today we know that eating me can prevent heart disease. My traditions are many, and my forms are many. Blessings to you now and always."

Take the corn goddess and straw man from the main altar and say:

"Blessings to you, grains of the world. We recognize your sacrifices so that we may not go hungry. We harvest you not with sadness at your death but with joy at the life you bring to us all. As we commit these figures to the flames, we send your spirits back that you may live again next spring, and we honor your sacrifice. The cycle goes ever onward. Blessings to you now and always, spirits of the grain."

Place the two figures in the flames, then lead everyone in the two-line chant "No End to the Circle" without the verses. Let it go where it may, either staying quiet or rising boisterously. When it's finished, move on to the cakes and ale, having the four grain priest/esses help distribute the food. When this is done, move on to the gift pouches by handing out the empty pouches and saying:

"You will be walking around the circle to receive gifts from each of the grain spirits. Please stand and face to your left, then open your pouch so that the grains may be poured inside. You can plant them or simply keep them as a reminder of their gifts to you."

Each priest/ess in turn puts a few kernels of grain into each person's pouch. When all have received their grains and come back to where they started, have them remain standing as you end the ritual.

"Grains of the Earth, of the East, the South, the West, the North . . . thank you for your blessings today and each day that we live. May we never forget how important you are to the world. Blessed Be."

Open the circle as desired, then say, "Merry meet, merry part, and merry meet again" or whatever ending is traditional for your group to indicate that the ritual is over. 🖉

Mabon Mothers

WHEN: Mabon

WHERE: Outside

CAST: HP/S, Harvest Mother, Dark Mother, Horned Lord

MINIMUM NUMBER OF PARTICIPANTS: Four

RITUAL DRESS: Harvest Mother dresses in muted greens and browns with a head wreath of wheat and grapes; Dark Mother dresses in black with a head wreath of black and winter greens with black feathers and spiders; Horned Lord dresses in furs and has an antler crown (or holds up a pair of antlers, or has a staff with antler top)

SUGGESTED SONGS: "Ancient Mother" (traditional), "Gaia Speaks" by Deborah Hamouris, "Hoof and Horn" by Ian Corrigan or "Horned One" by Buffalo, "Blood of the Ancients" by Ellen Klaver and Charlie Murphy, "She Changes Everything She Touches" by Starhawk, "We Are a Circle" by Rick Hamouris

PROPS: Reversible cape, black on one side with a glitter or beaded spider web and a harvest print on the other side, length of black or white gauze fabric to represent veil, at least one large pitcher of rose water (use about one cup of culinary rose water per gallon of distilled or spring water), large basket to hold Veil fabric, chair or stool next to the main altar for the Dark Mother

ALTAR SETUP: One main altar with the usual necessities

CAKES AND ALE: Whole wheat or multigrain baguettes (people tear off a piece) and wine or grape juice

NOTES: The potluck should be a generous harvest feast, featuring breads and seasonal foods like squash, rice, blackberries, grapes, and so on.

Perform basic housekeeping such as the five-minute warning chime, announcements, and so on. Cast the circle and call the four elements/guardians/directions as desired. Then say:

"We will now call to the Lady and Lord so that they may assist us in our important work today—cleansing the Veil between the worlds in preparation for Samhain."

You (or your designated singer) begin to sing "Ancient Mother" and indicate that everyone should join in. The woman portraying Her uses this time to invoke and put on the head wreath and harvest cape, then steps out into the center of the circle when ready. The Dark Mother should be mentally preparing as well. The Harvest Mother then sings "Gaia Speaks" as she looks meaningfully into the faces of everyone in the circle. When she has finished, she says:

> "Let us now call to my Lord, that he may answer and join us in the circle today."

She begins to sing "Hoof and Horn" (or "Horned One," your choice) and indicates that everyone should join in. As before, the man portraying Him uses this time to invoke, then steps out into the center of the circle when ready and dances or walks deosil, nodding to the people in the circle and looking into their faces, for one or two verses. At the end of the verse, the Mother stops singing and they embrace.

The Dark Mother dons the black head wreath and steps into the circle. The Harvest Mother breaks off the embrace and the Horned Lord steps back a few paces. Now begins the transfer of power:

> HM: "Who are you?"
>
> DM: "Why, don't you know me? It is fast becoming my time. I am She of winter and death . . . She of the cauldron and the crossroads."
>
> HM: "But it's still the time of the harvest. My Lord still feeds His people, and they are still reaping Him in."

> DM: "True, but He must die for the people to be fed."
>
> HM: "I preside over His death every year, but you are the one that brings it."
>
> DM: "That's right. Your time is at an end as mine is beginning. We must prepare."

The Harvest Mother hangs her head as if making a decision, then looks up at the Dark Mother and removes her cloak. She flips it over to reveal the black spider web side, and places it over the shoulders of the Dark Mother. They embrace, and the Harvest Mother stands beside the Horned Lord. The Dark Mother turns to the rest of the circle and says:

> "Before the new wheat can be stored, the storehouse must be swept clean. The Veil needs cleansing as well, before we ask for its help at Samhain. Over time, the Veil accumulates psychic energies, sustains injury due to ill magics, and must put up with all the physical and mental garbage that the mundane world throws at it every day. Let us now cleanse the Veil, that it may be healed, nurtured, and healthy for the coming times."

The Harvest Mother fades into the background during the Dark Mother's speech and removes the head wreath, placing it on the main altar. The Horned Lord steps forward and helps the Dark Mother unfurl the fabric that represents the Veil. The Horned Lord and Dark Mother hold opposite ends of the fabric. Pick up the pitcher of rose water and say:

"One at a time, we will be washing the Veil with a small amount of rose water from this pitcher. Let's all sing and send healing energies to the Veil as we do this important work."

Begin the chant (either "Blood of the Ancients" or "She Changes Everything She Touches," your choice) as you pour a bit of rose water over the fabric. Hand the pitcher to the person standing due east and indicate that they are to walk up and pour a bit over the fabric. Help everyone in turn until everyone in the circle has been able to wash the Veil. The Veil may be brought over to the disabled if necessary. If your crowd is large enough, use "She Changes Everything She Touches" with the counterpoint verses sprinkled in as people are moved to add them—it will definitely be one of those goosebump experiences. Clapping and simple drumming may be added, but keep the energy low and even for this working.

When everyone has had a chance to wash the Veil, proclaim:

"It is done! The Veil has been cleansed—now let us all offer our blessings and positive energies so that it may be ready for the winter to come."

The Dark Mother and Horned Lord carefully fold up the fabric and place it in the large basket, which is positioned in the middle of the circle. Begin the chant, either "Blood of the Ancients" if it was not used previously in the ritual, or "We Are a Circle." If in doubt, use the chant with which you think the group is more familiar. The Dark Mother starts the spiral dance, followed by the Horned Lord, Harvest Mother, you, and the rest of the participants. The disabled or any who wish to be in the center of the spiral should be assisted there as the spiral begins.

When the spiral has gone to the center and back out again to its end, and the chant has come back around to its end, the Dark Mother proclaims:

"We've done it! The Veil has been blessed, and we are now ready to prepare for winter. Now let us rejoice in the sacrifice of the Dying God and celebrate His gifts to us."

The Harvest Mother takes the wine or juice, the Horned Lord takes the bread, and you take around small paper cups for everyone. The Dark Mother takes the basket containing the Veil fabric and sets it before the main altar, where she is seated for the duration of the "cakes and ale." Announce that any who wish to seek the wisdom of the Dark Mother may approach Her and do so now. This time may be accompanied by pleasant music, or may be silent.

When everyone is ready, the Horned Lord and Harvest Mother stand on either side of the Dark Mother. Say:

"Everyone please join me in giving thanks to the Old Ones who have blessed us by being here today. Lady of the harvest, Lord of life and death, Lady of the darkness, we honor you today, and we thank you for your blessings and lessons. May you love us as we love you. We ask now that you depart from your servants so that they may enjoy the harvest feast we have laid in your honor. Go if you must, stay if you will. Hail and farewell."

The three people portraying the deities are given a bit of time to come back to themselves as needed (this time can also occur during the next section if desired or if the ritual is running long). Now say farewell to the four elements and open the circle in the same manner that it was cast. Say, "Merry meet, merry part, and merry meet again" or whatever ending is traditional for your group to indicate that the ritual is over.

Lammas Bread

WHEN: Lammas

WHERE: Outside

CAST: HP/S, bread tender, designated singer if necessary

MINIMUM NUMBER OF PARTICIPANTS: Two

RITUAL DRESS: Shades of brown and gold

SUGGESTED SONGS: "Turn Again" by Catherine Madsen, "Hoof and Horn" by Buffalo

PROPS: Covered barbecue with briquettes, flat pan (like a round cake pan or pie tin) of risen bread dough covered with a linen cloth

ALTAR SETUP: The usual necessities plus wheat sheaves, other grains, a gold altarcloth, barbecue off to one side where no one will bump it

CAKES AND ALE: The fresh bread from the ritual, beer/mead and rice milk or horchata

NOTES: Light your briquettes a half hour before the start of ritual so they have a chance to get to the right temperature and burn off any lighter fluid. The bread takes about twenty minutes to bake—to be sure of the timings, make a practice loaf and time the baking as well as the songs and meditation. Make sure your bread tender has made bread before and knows how to regulate the temperature of the barbecue so things turn out well. If the bread is done early, take it out when it's ready—it's better to cut short the meditation than have burned ritual bread.

Perform basic housekeeping such as announcements and so on. Cast the circle by sprinkling grains of wheat on the ground before you and saying:

"We bless this circle, and surround ourselves with the power of the God who has given his life that we may be fed, and the Goddess whose bounty sustains us. The circle is cast . . . so mote it be."

Call the elements, starting in the East:

"Morning star, winds of change, rising sun . . . we call to you. Bring us your wisdom and perspective. Hail and welcome.

"Heart of the sun, fires that bake the bread . . . we call to you. Bring us your courage and strength. Hail and welcome.

"Waters of life, oceans of love and mystery . . . we call to you. Bring us your patience and hope. Hail and welcome.

"Crystal caves, beautiful darkness, midnight sun . . . we call to you. Bring us your mysteries and magic. Hail and welcome."

Next give a brief introduction to Lammas:

"This is the time of both life and death . . . the time when the sun's power enters the grain for the first time . . . the time when Demeter grieves for her daughter . . . the time that the grain must die so that the people may live. 'Lammas' is short for 'loaf mass,' the time when the Christian church bakes sacred loaves, but this festival is pre-Christian and is also called Lughnassadh [*luna-sah*] in honor of the Celtic god Lugh [*loo*], the Golden One, master of all arts, the corn king.

"Some also say that 'Lammas' is actually short for 'Lugh mass,' dating from when the church took over the Pagan rituals where Lugh defeated Crom Dubh [crom doo], becoming rituals where the clergy defeated the Pagan Crom Dubh, and up until 1993 when it was stolen, an ancient stone head of Crom Dubh was part of an early ruined Christian church in Ireland, mingling Christianity with the ancient Pagan practice of keeping the head of your slain enemy in your fort to keep his power.

"So today we call to Lugh, the Golden One, and Crom Dubh, the one whose back is bent from carrying the blessed wheat sheaves to feed humankind. Bring us the power of the sun, the mysteries of the underworld, and the golden wheat that we may survive the winter once again. Hail, and welcome."

Move over to the bread dough, carefully pick it up, and uncover it. Bless it and empower it, then place the uncovered dough with care into the barbecue with the help of your bread tender. Place the lid on the barbecue, then sing "Turn Again" at a relaxed pace, encouraging everyone to sing along on the chorus (use a designated singer if you need to).

Begin the meditation while the bread bakes, reading as slowly as necessary to ensure that the bread is ready at the right time:

"Be comfortable and close your eyes. Relax . . . take a deep breath . . . and let it out . . . let your worries pass through your fingers like sand . . . breathe deeply again . . . and let it out . . . and find yourself in a meadow, under the bright sunny sky. You smell the green grasses and the moist, black soil under your feet . . . you walk through the endless green field and the grass becomes taller . . . you brush it with your hands as you walk, the sun becoming higher in the sky.

"Breathe in the fragrance of fresh growing things . . . listen to the bird songs . . . the blackbird, the meadowlark, the goldfinch . . . and still the grass grows . . . like hair, wild and bushy, waving in the winds that caress your skin. . . .

"The sun is getting lower now, but hotter. The grass grows taller still, and you see that it is an endless field of wheat that surrounds you. Far in the distance you see some figures working . . . and the wheat ripens around you as you continue to walk. The sun dips a little lower, and the wheat starts to become golden yellow around you, the stiff beards of the ripening grain heads brushing against your arms and body. You sense now that these living plants are dying, but they die because it is their time . . . there is no sorrow at their sacrifice . . . it is simply their way. They sigh as you pass . . . touching you in both greeting and farewell . . . and you bless them in return.

"You walk toward the figures in the distance and see that they are working hard. They are the reapers . . . they see you now and welcome you, giving you a golden scythe so that you may take your place among them. The dry grasses whisper in the breeze around you . . . what do they say? *(pause)*

"Before you cut, you give thanks to the grasses for their sacrifice, and the people stop and listen to your words. What do you say? *(pause)*

"Now you begin to cut the wheat. You fall into a rhythm . . . back and forth . . . back and forth . . . cutting the grain . . . back and forth . . . always cutting . . . the sun setting . . . the light golden as it goes into the grain . . . back and forth . . . how long has it been . . .? Hours . . .? Days . . .? Forever it seems . . . you cut, back and forth. . . .

"The rhythm entrances you, and your body works by itself in the tall, endless wheat field . . . your vision blurs, and your body continues the rhythm as your mind finds itself in front of two men, one tall, with blond hair and a spear, the other short, with dark hair and a back bent under the weight of a huge sheaf of wheat. They are Lugh the Golden and Crom Dubh, and they have a gift and a message for you. *(pause—at least a minute)*

"You thank these Lords of the Grain, and give them a gift in return." (pause about thirty seconds) "You look up at the sky, which has turned golden with the setting sun, and realize that your body is still cutting the wheat . . . back and forth . . . when you look back down, you are back in the wheat field again with your fellow reapers . . . cutting . . . back and forth . . . but you grow thirsty and finally put your scythe down so that the harvesters and gleaners can bundle up the wheat into sheaves.

"You turn and see a wooden cart with some sheaves inside, and a boy beckons you over, a cup of cold, clear water in his hands. You drink, and no water has ever tasted better. The last few drops you pour onto the ground in libation, then you return the cup and the boy winks his wheat-colored eye at you.

"Your job is done . . . now it is time to celebrate the God and his gifts to you. You stride back into the wheat, walking back the way you came . . . through the stubble where the stalks have been cut . . . through the whole grasses yet

to be harvested . . . toward the golden orange sunset . . . feeling the first hints of cool evening descend . . . you breathe deeply and begin to return . . . take another deep breath and feel yourself come back to this circle . . . to this place of magic to celebrate the God of the grain. Take another deep breath, and, when you are ready, be here now."

Check with your bread tender on the progress of the loaf, and plan the next section accordingly— if the bread is done, bring it out when everyone has returned and chant for a couple of minutes. If it is not done, chant and drum, perhaps adding freeform dancing (on the opposite side of the circle from the barbecue for safety) as long as necessary until the bread is ready.

Lead everyone in the chant "Hoof and Horn," building it up and sending the energy into the bread. When the chant has concluded and the bread is done, move into cakes and ale, letting people tear off hunks of the hot bread and going around the circle until it's all gone. Remember to save some for yourself, for the bread tender, and to give some back to the Earth with the libation.

Begin closing down the ritual with the libation, saying:

"Gods of the grain, bright and dark, Lords of the mysteries of life and death, we give you this offering. . . . We feed you as you feed us. . . . Take this nourishment and live again as the wheel turns to winter and then the spring. Blessed be."

Now dismiss the elements and open the circle:

"Dark mysteries of the North, we thank you for your lessons, insights, and magic. Hail and farewell.

"Sacred waters of the West, we thank you for your love, empathy, and patience. Hail and farewell.

"Eternal flame of the South, we thank you for your strength, power, and will. Hail and farewell.

"Invisible winds of the East, we thank you for your changes, hope, and wisdom. Hail and farewell.

"I open this circle and release the sacred grains to the earth, that they may spring green and renew the cycle of life evermore. Let us release these mysteries into the world, that we shall never forget the gifts given to us by the Lord. So mote it be."

Say, "Merry meet, merry part, and merry meet again" or whatever ending is traditional for your group to indicate that the ritual is over.

The Wealth of Lakshmi

WHEN: October or early November (check a Hindu calendar for this year's dates of either Navaratri or Diwali—both festivals are the traditional time to honor Lakshmi)
WHERE: Indoors or Outdoors
CAST: HP/S
MINIMUM NUMBER OF PARTICIPANTS: One
RITUAL DRESS: Red, green, or white robes (all should be dressed in the same color)

SUGGESTED SONGS: Hindu mantra/meditation, such as "Lakshmi" by Sri Siva or some of the chant CDs by Robert Gass and On Wings of Song
PROPS: *Tingshas* or energy chime, basket of votive or tealight candles and a large platter of sand to hold them when lit, coins (Indian coins are especially good) or small gifts, conch shell horn, coconut, wooden cutting board, ice pick

or clean screwdriver, hammer, cup for the coconut water, bowl or basket for the coconut pieces

ALTAR SETUP: One large main altar with a statue of Lakshmi, necklaces to adorn the statue (such as a lotus seed mala, strand of pearls, and so on), sandalwood oil, fresh flowers, incense, special candle (lotus-shaped is ideal or use a lotus-shaped holder), "cakes and ale," matches

CAKES AND ALE: Any traditional Indian bread and milk or soymilk

NOTES: Lakshmi is especially fond of sweets—if you will be having a potluck, you can make it "desserts only" for fun. Warn your guests that beef is strictly forbidden for this potluck—the Hindu sacred cow is the earthly incarnation of Lakshmi and is offered special veneration at this time—it would be a grave insult to Her to eat a dead cow at Her *puja*! However, milk products are not only acceptable, they are preferred as they embody the sacred milk of Lakshmi. Also encourage everyone to bring drums, bells, and other rhythm instruments.

Perform basic housekeeping such as announcements and so on. Give a brief explanation of the ritual:

"Lakshmi [*lock-shmee*] is a well-known Hindu deity. She is a beautiful goddess, one of the three aspects of Durga [*der-gah*], the Great Mother. Lakshmi represents the aspect of wealth, and is often shown with coins flowing from two of her four hands; in her other hands she holds the lotus, which indicates spiritual wealth. Lakshmi represents all the forms of riches in your life, including family, material possessions, knowledge, accomplishment . . . I'm sure you can think of many more. We will be exploring this idea more today and honoring Lakshmi through *puja* [*poo-jah*], which means 'worship' or 'celebration.' So now let's prepare ourselves and our sacred space."

Cense and asperge all participants, accompanied by your favorite appropriate chant (such as "Air I Am") or play soothing Indian music. Cast the circle simply, perhaps with a ring of salt, incense, rice, or rose water, either in silence or saying something like:

"With this salt [or incense, etc.] I purify this sacred space. . . . May all we do within this circle be pure and perfect, in love and beauty."

Ring the *tingshas*, the traditional Hindu signal of the beginning of meditation. Light the lotus candle and incense before the goddess statue, then turn to the other participants and say:

"Some say that Lakshmi has always existed, floating before creation on a lotus. Some say that She emerged from the milky foam of the sea bedecked with jewels, the perfect embodiment of beauty, grace, and wealth. As Shri [*shree*] Lakshmi, she is the active female Shakti [*shock-tee*] energy of Lord Vishnu [*vish-new*]. She is also called Mata [*mah-tah*] Lakshmi, meaning "Mother Lakshmi," because she is one of the aspects of Durga, the Great Mother of the Hindus.

"It is now that the goddess returns to earth, and it is said that on the full-moon night of Diwali [*dih-wall-ee*] She waits invisible along the roads and around our homes, bestowing riches and granting wishes to the faithful who live good lives.

"In giving, one receives. That is why *puja* includes giving food, sandalwood, light, adornments, and other offerings to the deity—it would be greedy and selfish to beg for favors without giving anything back."

Now wash the statue of Lakshmi, then dab on sandalwood oil, then adorn the statue, all the while speaking to Her during the offerings ("I wash you that you may be pure and cleansed, I offer you sweet sandalwood . . ." and so on. Use whatever words feel right to you). This also helps the audience get more of a sense of what is happening if they are unfamiliar with puja. Finally say:

"*Om Sri Maha Lakshmiyei Swaha!*" [*ohm shree mah-ha lock-shmee-yay swa-ha!*]

This can be declared enthusiastically, or can be intoned slowly like a chant or mantra. Sound the conch horn, then announce:

"Let us honor Lakshmi with drumming and dancing! Let us send Her our love and blessings!"

You, or designated drummers and dancers, begin the music and dancing, encouraging everyone to join in. Those without instruments are encouraged to clap along. Keep a close watch on the energy peak and signal the release of the energy to Lakshmi by walking over to the altar and/or signaling the drummers to conclude. Stand before the altar and channel the energy to Lakshmi.

When the moment is right and it is relatively quiet in the room, begin to chant "Om," encouraging participation if necessary. Continue the Om chant until the room is balanced and hangs on that one perfect sound, then let it die away gently. Pause a moment, then gently say:

"The wealth of the moment. The glory of being alive, in balance, witnessing perfection. Wealth has many meanings and many faces. Close your eyes now and think about the wealth in your own life. Your friends . . . your family . . . your home . . . your accomplishments . . . your pets . . . your garden . . . your spirituality . . . the things that bring you joy. Think not about what you wish you had, think now about what you do have. Allow Lakshmi to come to you, to reveal to you the wealth in your life. (*Pause for about a minute.*)

"As you are ready, come up to the altar one by one. Light a candle, and declare the wealth in your life. You will receive a gift from Lakshmi to remind you that wealth is more than money. Wealth is everything around you that makes you happy."

You go first, lighting a candle and declaring out loud your personal wealth. Remain next to the altar and give a coin or gift to each person who comes up to light a candle.

When everyone has lit a candle and received a gift, say:

> "Behold Lakshmi, goddess of all wealth! Let us now partake of the sacred offerings—what we have given to Lakshmi she now shares with us. If you wish to come up to the altar and speak with Lakshmi privately, this is a perfect time."

Distribute the bread and milk, enlisting help from others if you are the lone HP/S. When everyone has finished eating and/or visiting the altar, ring the *tingshas* again. Place the coconut on the cutting board and say:

> "The coconut represents birth from the fertilized egg, and it can also be seen as representing fulfillment—in this case, it represents the completion of our ritual. As you leave, take a piece of this coconut with you as a gift from Lakshmi. You can enjoy eating it fresh off the shell, or you can dry it and save it for later puja to Lakshmi in your home."

Punch a hole in the coconut through one of the dark "eyes" with the ice pick or screwdriver, and pour the milk out into a cup that is placed on the altar (pour it onto the ground when taking down the altar, or you can save it and use it for sacred purposes later). The coconut is then broken with the hammer into enough pieces for everyone and the pieces are placed in a dish or basket on the altar. You can enlist a helper for this if necessary. Then say:

> "I release this sacred space and open it so that Lakshmi's blessings of wealth, beauty, and enlightenment may encircle us and the world. Blessings to Lakshmi, and blessings to everyone here. Let us now enjoy our feast!"

Acknowledge Lakshmi, then lead everyone over to the buffet table to enjoy the potluck.

IV

WINTER

Earth Teacher

WHEN: Winter

WHERE: Outside if possible, or indoors

CAST: HP and HPS (or HP/S and helper), at least two good singers

MINIMUM NUMBER OF PARTICIPANTS: Two

RITUAL DRESS: Robes or dresses in shades of green and neutral colors

SUGGESTED SONGS: "Round and Round" by Libana, "See the Earth Is Turning" by Adele Getty

PROPS: Besom, song lyrics for everyone if needed, a basket of small crystal points to give to everyone

ALTAR SETUP: One large main altar in the north of the area with the necessities, including a candle for each direction

CAKES AND ALE: something earthy

Perform basic housekeeping such as announcements and so on.

Sweep the circle and cast it at the same time with a besom as the helper follows, sprinkling salt to form the circle's boundaries. You can use your own words, or slowly say:

"Be cleansed, circle of art. Be purified, circle of magic. Be blessed, circle of earth. This place is sacred. This place is holy. This place is between the worlds."

The helper picks up a frame drum with beater and begins to play a slow, single, steady beat. Walk to the main altar, pick up the East candle, and face East, saying:

"Spirits of the East, the place of new beginnings, help us to remember your blessings, help us hold on to the hope that spring will return soon and the Earth will bloom again. Hail and welcome."

The candle is lit and replaced on the altar. The South candle is held up to the South, and you say:

"Spirits of the South, the place of power and fire, help us to remember your blessings, help us remember what the heat of the summer sun feels like on our cold faces. Help awaken the Earth. Hail and welcome."

The candle is lit and replaced on the altar. The West candle is held up to the West, and you say:

"Spirits of the West, the place of fulfillment and the tears of emotion, help us to remember your blessings, frozen though they may be, stormy though they may be, help us bless the Earth. Hail and welcome."

The HP/S lights the candle and places it back on the altar, taking up the North candle now. Face North and say:

"Spirits of the North, of the frozen wastes, the place of rest and remembrance, of green things and of death, help us remember your blessings as we honor the Earth today. Come and be with us now. Hail and welcome."

Light the candle and replace it on the main altar. Turn around abruptly, cueing the drummers to stop. Silence reigns for a moment as you remain motionless. Cue the singer with a gesture, then, quietly at first, one voice begins to sing "Round and Round" (if you are the singer, simply begin to sing). On the third time through, another voice takes up the round, coming in on "turning always." If there are more singers, have them come in on subsequent cycles so that the song lasts about a minute or so. After the last voice has concluded the song, allow a few moments of silence, then begin the meditation:

"Be comfortable and close your eyes. We are now in the dark time of the year, the time when some animals hibernate in burrows deep underground, the time when the autumn seeds lay upon the ground but cannot sprout yet. The winter brings the uncanny stillness of the snow, a colorless world of branches and stones, featureless gray skies, and spaces of timelessness . . . moments frozen in ice as if the whole world is waiting for something.

"Relax your body with a few deep breaths . . . and feel your spine . . . the bones that hold you up like the bones of a tree . . . feel your tailbone reaching toward the earth, a reminder of your connection to the animal world . . . feel the kundalini serpent energy of your genitals echoing the fertility of the earth, ever reaching toward each other. Reach downward with your spine and your kundalini energy, down into the earth, putting down roots . . . roots that become you.

"You are inside your own roots, reaching . . . reaching down . . . slipping inside the earth, between the stones, between the other roots, between the sleeping animals and insects . . . deeper . . . and deeper. . . .

"Inside the earth you begin to feel warmer as you reach past the bedrock . . . past the shell of the earth . . . you begin to touch the lava that holds up the earth's skin but it does not burn. You explore this liquid fire, going deeper still . . . from red, to yellow, to the earth's heart of white fire. You dance in the flames, in the light, and you feel renewed.

"You linger for a moment . . . then you slowly begin to rise up from the flames, a phoenix who knows the earth's heart. You rise back up through the yellow . . . orange . . . and red magma until you reach the crust and break through . . . where you find yourself at the bottom of the ocean.

"You are not afraid, for you have no need for air in your spirit form. The cool waters refresh you as you swim and float, a nice change from the heat at the core. You look up and see the surface far above and begin to float upwards, up toward the sky far above, up with the small bubbles of air formed by the plants and animals that call the ocean home. Through the water you can see clouds far above, and you break through the surface to feel the winds caress you.

"In your spirit form you drift free, soaring up like the eagle, riding the thermals ever upward in the air that dries you, leaving behind the salts of the ocean so that your body is purified. As you fly higher and higher you can begin to see the curved horizon of the earth, and the sky above you becomes darker as you ascend. Higher still you climb, up into the atmosphere, past the layer of air that sustains life on this planet. You pause and see the earth far below you, and you marvel at it. . . . *(pause)*

"You know now that the earth is everything. It is the stone under your feet. It is the fire in the heart. It is the waters of life. It is the air you breathe. *(pause)*

"You begin to descend, understanding this truth, looking at all the features of the earth as you glide downward. You see the clouds below you . . . you see the oceans reflecting sunlight . . . you see mountains and forests and the works of humankind. You descend back into our circle . . . back into your body . . . and as you come back into your body, feel your bones . . . feel your body's moisture . . . feel your heat and life returning . . . feel the air in your lungs. For you are a perfect reflection of the earth. And, as you are ready, open your eyes and be here now."

Allow a few moments for everyone to return and open their eyes. Begin to sing "See the Earth Is Turning" and encourage people to join in. When the group is singing strongly, motion for everyone to stand and join hands in a circle. When all are singing and standing, begin a slow spiral dance in time to the song. Keep it slow and steady, try to avoid a "crack the whip" effect if possible. When the spiral has concluded and all are standing in a circle again, join hands with the last person in line and end the song. Now say:

"We have woven new possibilities. We have honored the earth and helped to turn the wheel a bit closer to the hope of spring. We are the weavers of magic . . . what we do is sacred."

Move to the altar and get the basket of crystal points, then say:

"May these gifts of the earth remind you that the earth is all the elements together, including spirit. These crystals are made of hard quartz, but they reach out to the spirit world as well. The earth is not an absolute . . . the earth is everything we imagine and more . . . the earth is perhaps our greatest teacher and gift giver."

Give a crystal to each participant, then bless the cakes and ale. You and any helpers then pass out the refreshments to all and allow five or ten minutes for people to relax, eat, and discuss the ritual. After any trash is gathered up, stand in the center to begin closing the ritual. Beginning in the North, thank and dismiss the elements as they were called, blowing out the candles in turn, then open the circle as desired.

Say, "Merry meet, merry part, and merry meet again" or whatever ending is traditional for your group to indicate that the ritual is over. ❧

Black Light Chaos

WHEN: Samhain

WHERE: Inside

CAST: HP/S, four elemental priest/esses

MINIMUM NUMBER OF PARTICIPANTS: Five

RITUAL DRESS: Your choice—be aware of how your outfit will react in the black light; decide whether you want to glow or not, and adjust accordingly (tip: lint will appear from another dimension all over dark clothing). The elemental priest/esses should have black leotards on underneath their ritual clothing, or, even better, skeleton suits. Their ritual wear for the chaos section is very basic white UV-reactive skull makeup, "mystery hoods" with black scrim in front of the face, and the black leotards—make sure people know how to apply their makeup in advance to avoid any delays, and make sure they keep it very simple to save time.

SUGGESTED SONGS: Something strange and "new-agey" without any real beat (about three to four minutes long), "All Souls Night" by Loreena McKennitt

PROPS: Skeleton props (see above and below), assorted candles encircling the room for basic lighting, CD player, fog machine, UV bubbles and bubble machine, oil wheel projector, other party lighting effects (all optional, but try to get at least one or two of these).

ALTAR SETUP: A small altar for each direction, such as a folding wooden TV tray, containing a candle, matches, and small altarcloth for each direction.

CAKES AND ALE: *Pan de muertos*—traditional Mexican bone-shaped bread; ale, and sparkling apple cider or mulled hot apple cider

NOTES: The smaller the room, the better and more intense the black-light effect will be. For a room that's about 15 ft. x 15 ft., a three-foot fluorescent black-light tube will be about right if placed in the center of the room. You can use ordinary fluorescent light fixtures and simply replace the regular tube with a black-light tube for the least expensive method of doing this. Conceal the fixtures behind some lightweight black netting fabric or black theatrical scrim until you're ready to light them so it's a total surprise. Also be sure to hide any lighting and fog effects, taking off the covering when the meditation is over so that they can operate properly. (Follow all

instructions regarding fire safety and use safe coverings for the machines, especially those that get hot.) You will also need a secluded changing area for the skeletons, one with room for four people, their costumes and makeup, a small light, and a mirror for applying the skull makeup.

Perform basic housekeeping such as announcements and so on. Give a brief explanation of the ritual:

"Tonight we will take a journey. Usually, on Samhain, this means taking a journey to the Summerland . . . Avalon . . . the place of our ancestors and decendants. But tonight we will walk a different path beyond the Veil. We will visit the Underworld . . . the primordial chaos from which all was formed, and to which all must return. For this, we must weave our circle tightly . . . we don't want anyone left behind when it's time to come back."

Cast the circle three times, and end by grounding the tool in the earth (or touching it to the floor). When you are satisfied that the circle is tight and solid enough, nod to the East priest/ess as the cue to begin calling the elements, lighting a candle for each:

"Guardians of the Watchtowers of the East, come guard this circle and all present here. Hail and welcome."

This is repeated for South, West, and North by those priest/esses, who then begin to light the other candles around the room. One of them turns off the hall lights, leaving only candles for illumination. The priest/esses exit to put on their skeleton makeup and costumes. Now give a guided meditation (read slowly so the skeletons have plenty of time to change):

"Close your eyes, be comfortable, and relax. We are going to travel . . . Take a deep breath, hold it for a moment . . . and let it go. Take another deep breath . . . and a third . . . letting all your mundane troubles and worries go as you let the air leave your body.

"Air is one of the four elements we honor and call upon in our rituals. Fire is another, and we find fire in ourselves, too . . . the body heat we produce as well as our will to make things happen. Water is here, too, in your blood, in your saliva . . . and of course Earth makes up our bones, our hair, and the other solid bits of our bodies. Remember this as we travel together. Take a moment now to feel the four elements inside yourself, and connect to each Guardian in turn, for they will guide and protect you. *(Pause about a minute, using this time to blow out all but the four directional candles and uncover the lighting and fog effect machines.)*

"Now take another deep breath and let it go, feeling yourself becoming distant from this room. You begin to feel the ground disappear, but you are not disoriented, you are simply floating away from the mundane world . . . separate from ordinary reality . . . seeking . . . ever seeking . . . looking for something that will tell you which way to go. You seek the path of magic . . . you seek the path of truth . . . you seek the path of healing yourself . . . so let us see what we can find.

"You float, looking around with your mind's eye until you see nothing but darkness before you, behind you, all around you. You float in this darkness, but you are not afraid, for this is the place between places . . . this is the Mother's womb . . . this is Hecate's cauldron. Remember what it was like to be inside your mother's womb . . . so safe, so dark, so comforting. *(pause)*

"Now you notice a bit of light below you. Not a bright light, but not the total darkness of the womb. You float a bit closer to the light . . . what could it be? As curious as a child, you float closer still . . . dark shapes move in the dim, swirling light below you. You begin to realize that you are actually floating inside not air, but water . . . don't worry, you are a part of this place and a part of the elements . . . the Guardians will protect you, keep you safe.

"You move a bit closer and begin to hear a few strange sounds. *(Begin warming up the fogger and any lighting effects at this point, putting fog into the room when the machine is ready.)* You encounter some strange smells . . . you get closer and things brush up against your skin . . . there's a taste you don't recognize in the air . . . the lights move and change, shifting and rippling like sunlight through the surface of the water. Where are you? Can you find your way back? *(Pause—finish getting the room ready and cue the strange "new-agey" music, which is the cue for the four priest/esses to come back in.)*

"Now, open your eyes and see just where you are . . . inside the Underworld, the primordial chaos of possibilities. . . . Will you dance inside the waters?"

The skeletons get everyone up and slowly dancing to the strange music. When the music changes to "All Souls Night," the skeletons remove their hoods on the first few drum beats (about thirty seconds into the song), toss them to you, and help get everyone started on a deosil spiral dance (don't try to corral people too much—when people figure out what's happening, everyone will join in). Try to time out the pacing of the spiral in advance so that it ends approximately when the song ends. If it's done before the music is over, just keep everyone circling deosil.

Now say:

"We have made order from chaos! Now take that energy and create order in your own life from the ocean of possibilities. Give some back to the Mother . . . send some to your loved ones, keep some for yourself. . . . Whatever you need to do with it, this creative energy is from the Source . . . use it wisely.

"Please rest now, and be seated. We have done our work, and we need to return to manifest the magic in our lives. Please close your eyes and prepare."

The priest/esses return to the dressing room once people have closed their eyes; meanwhile, you re-light the candles and turn off the effects machines during the meditation.

"Breathe deeply and feel your body around you. Feel the energy that you bring back with you . . . what will you use it for, and what does it look like? *(pause)* Remember where you've put it so that you can draw it out later as you need to.

"Breathe again; as you look around, you see four lights that stand together. These are the guardians of the watchtowers, and they will guide you home . . . the lights begin to move, and you follow them. They move upward, back through the total darkness of the Mother's womb . . . pausing for just a moment so that you may rest. *(pause)*

"The lights move onward, separating and moving so that they surround you, one light in each direction. You begin to feel the floor underneath you again, sense the mundane curtain of daily reality descending slowly around you as you sit. . . . You breathe deeply again as the four lights of the guardians become candle flames . . . and when you are ready, you may open your eyes to return fully to your body . . . return to our ritual space."

Serve the cakes and ale, asking for help from among the crowd if the priest/esses are not yet out of their makeup and back into their ritual robes. Allow about five to eight minutes for people to chat and relax as they ground themselves with the food and drink. When people are done eating and the cups and napkins have been gathered, the North priest/ess stands, waits for everyone else to stand, and begins the dismissals:

"Guardians of the Watchtowers of the North, we thank you for helping us and guiding us back home. Go if you must, stay if you will. Hail and farewell."

This is repeated for West, South, and East by those priest/esses, who also extinguish their candles in turn. Open the circle in the same manner that it was cast, then say, "Merry meet, merry part, and merry meet again" or whatever ending is traditional for your group to indicate that the ritual is over. ❧

Dancing with the Ancestors

WHEN: Samhain
WHERE: Inside
CAST: HP/S, Challenger, drummer(s)
MINIMUM NUMBER OF PARTICIPANTS: Three
RITUAL DRESS: Your choice
SUGGESTED SONGS: "Breaths" by Sweet Honey in the Rock, "Old Ones" by Earl Edward Bates,

"Blood of the Ancients" by Ellen Klaver and Charlie Murphy
PROPS: Smoke machine, black cloth (if needed to form tunnel), black light and UV-reactive makeup for Challenger, chair for Challenger if needed, loads of assorted candles for along the walls of the second room

ALTAR SETUP: Main ancestor altar off to one side, the North is probably best for this depending on your tradition and site's limitations

CAKES AND ALE: Your choice—something hearty and nourishing is probably best, such as whole-wheat bread and hot spiced apple cider

NOTES: Have all bring something to remind them of their ancestors for the main altar.

The main ritual location must have a hallway that leads to another room big enough to accommodate everyone, or have a place to create an artificial tunnel or hallway with black cloth. Mount the black light over where the Challenger will be and use UV-reactive makeup to lend a frightening appearance. You can use the smoke machine at this location or near the entrance to the second room.

Before the ritual begins, the Challenger should be hidden in the hallway, but close enough to the first ritual room to hear the cue for the drummers, who should then be cued in turn.

Perform basic housekeeping such as announcements and so on. Have everyone be seated and give a short grounding:

"Close your eyes . . . take a deep breath . . . and see only darkness. Breathe in the blessed darkness . . . breathe out the blessed darkness. . . .

"In the darkness many mysteries are found . . . many things are hidden . . . and still other things are lost. In the darkness we rest, ready to begin anew. In the darkness we have no form, no skin color, no hair color, no clothing, nothing to judge each other by. Let the darkness brush over you like black velvet.

"Here in this blessed darkness the ancestors live, ready to come forth when they are needed. Now prepare yourself to enter this place. . . . Take a deep breath . . . and as you are ready, open your eyes and prepare to work magic."

Cense and asperge each person, working deosil around the group and using a helper if need be. When this has been completed, offer a short explanation of what will be happening:

"Today we take a journey. We will go to the land of the ancestors . . . to the Underworld . . . to the place where mysteries live. We will be traveling into darkness and back out again, and the path will be challenging, but together we will make it. As long as you are ready, and your heart is pure, you will pass through safely to the other side. Let us begin the journey."

This is the cue for the drummers to begin in the second room, starting with a slow, steady beat or heartbeat rhythm. Lead the procession very slowly down the corridor and come to the Challenger, who asks "Is your heart pure?" Say yes, and pass on slowly without looking back, thus showing the next person in line what to do. When you reach the next room, begin free-form dancing, encouraging everyone who enters to dance as well. When everyone is in the room, have the drummers soften until they are barely audible, then proclaim:

"Here we will dance with the ancestors! Let us raise energy for them, let us show them that we love them and value their guidance. Now!"

On this cue, the drummers begin a much more complex beat, gradually speeding it up until you signal that the energy has peaked (usually about two or three minutes). Ground your energy, showing others that they are to ground as well and be seated. Now give a short meditation:

"My friends, we have danced with the ancestors and they are with us now. But since they are still beyond the veil of death, we need to be very still and quiet to hear what they have to tell us.

"Breathe deeply and center yourself. It is still dark here, but the lights of their spirits show us the way. You feel your ancestors close to you . . . listen now. . . . What do they tell you . . . ?"

Allow several minutes for people to meditate and receive their messages, then quietly say, "Our time is short. Say goodbye to your ancestors, and prepare to return." Allow another minute or so, then have people take a deep breath or two and open their eyes. When you stand up (or point, or nod, or some other silent prearranged signal), this is the cue for the drummers to begin the slow, steady beat once again.

Slowly lead everyone back out into the corridor. The Challenger is still there, but merely watches everyone intensely as they pass by. As people enter the first room, indicate silently that they are to be seated once again. When everyone is back, give a short grounding:

"Breathe deeply the Air . . . feel the Fire in your blood . . . taste the Water in your mouth . . . sense the Earth in your bones . . . know that you are alive. Know that you yet walk the Earth on this side of the Veil.

"There is much work to do, and so we listen to the ancestors who know things we cannot know. Remember their words well . . . honor their gifts to us. Let us eat and drink in their honor and pay our respects at the ancestor altar."

Serve the food and drink to everyone, then be sure to go up and leave an offering at the ancestor altar. When all have finished paying their respects and eating, lead the group in the song "Breaths" or in the chant "Old Ones," or "Blood of the Ancients." Say, "Merry meet, merry part, and merry meet again" or whatever ending is traditional for your group to indicate that the ritual is over. 🪶

Ritual of the Drums

WHEN: Winter

WHERE: Outside or inside

CAST: HP/S, four directional priest/esses, drumming leader (optional, should be experienced at leading drum circles or rituals)

MINIMUM NUMBER OF PARTICIPANTS: Five

RITUAL DRESS: Your choice

PROPS: Instruments to represent the elements (see below), a bowl of fine sea salt, purification incense such as frankincense and myrrh, sandalwood, sage, and so on

ALTAR SETUP: One main altar with all the usual ritual tools for your group and four directional altars with the instruments to be used in the element invocations

CAKES AND ALE: Your choice of hearty bread and drink

NOTES: Have participants bring their own drums and instruments from home to be blessed

Perform basic housekeeping such as announcements and so on. Begin with a brief history of drums and their use:

"The use of drums stretches back into prehistoric times. No one knows what the first drums may have sounded like or how they were used. Were they hollow logs thumped with a branch to signal others? Were they frames covered with tight skins used to make music or for ritual purposes only? We may never know, but the forms and sounds of drums and other rhythm instruments have changed and grown through the eons.

"Some of the drums we use today are the same as they were thousands of years ago, such as the Native American frame drum or Egyptian tambourine; some are recent inventions, such as the steel drums of the Caribbean, and some are a blend of the two, such as the ancient Celtic *bodhran* [*bore-ahn*] that uses a modern tunable synthetic drum head.

"And let's not forget all the other rhythm instruments, like claves [*clah-vays*], rattles and shakers of every possible type, bells, gongs, spoons or bones, castanets, clappers, and on and on . . . it's quite a list! Today we celebrate these instruments that enhance our rituals and our lives."

You and a helper begin to cense and asperge everyone in the circle and the area as a single *dumbek* is played in a rhythm of your choice. The *dumbek* stops, whereupon you cast the circle as you normally do.

Beginning in the East, the elements are called with instruments only—in this case you and the East priest/ess use bells and rattles while concentrating on bringing the element of Air through the instruments. The same is done in the South with claves and other sharp clapper instruments played by you and the South priest/ess, the West with a rainstick, shell rattle and *dumbek*, and finally in the North with frame drums (the deeper the sound, the better). If desired, call upon the God and Goddess to attend the rite.

You and a helper take the bowl of fine sea salt and the purification incense and stand in the center of the circle. Say:

"We love our drums and instruments, and we use them in sacred ritual. As holy tools, they should be blessed with the love we would give to any other things we use in ritual regularly. If you wish to have your drum blessed and purified now in this sacred space, please come forward."

Say an appropriate blessing and sprinkle a pinch of salt over the instrument as each person comes forward. The incense smoke is also wafted over the instrument thoroughly. When all have come forward, you replace the salt and the helper replaces the incense.

You or the drumming leader now says:

"*Where the Wild Things Are* is a classic children's book where Max, in his wolf suit, goes to the land of the wild things and becomes their king. He then declares, 'LET THE WILD RUMPUS START!!'"

The lead drummer now starts playing a strong but simple rhythm, and any cast members who are not playing an instrument or who are using a small hand instrument begin to free-form dance and encourage everyone who wishes to do the same. Seated drummers should be encouraged to drum along as well, and the drumming leader should remain highly visible and keep eye contact with other strong drummers in the circle if possible. Allow the free-form dancing to continue about four minutes or so or until people are obviously growing tired, then allow the energy to peak and conclude.

When people seem lightly grounded and ready for more, the lead drummer begins a slower rhythm that can flow and ebb, but should maintain a slower, more relaxed pace than the previous dance. He or she can also shout "Let's have another!" or "Drum with me!" or similar if people aren't picking up on the fact that it's another free-form drumming session. Allow to taper off gently when the group is ready.

Now give a grounding meditation:

"Be seated, lay your instruments down gently, and close your eyes for a journey. We aren't going very far . . . *(Drum leader begins playing a heartbeat rhythm very softly.)* . . . but we need to see where the heartbeat is coming from.

"Feel the ground underneath you, and feel your energy reach out to the Earth. You feel yourself sinking down into the soil . . . down into the rocks . . . down past the tree roots and crawling things . . . until finally you find yourself in a small tunnel under the Earth where it is absolutely dark. Your back is against the end of the tunnel, and you reach out on either side of you to feel the tunnel walls. The heartbeat is coming from ahead of you, so you begin to walk slowly down the tunnel, letting your hands run along the walls.

"After a short time, you begin to realize that there's a very dim light ahead of you illuminating the tunnel . . . you can just start to make out a few rocks and roots in the distance. You keep walking, following the light . . . following the heartbeat. . . . It's warm down here, warm and cozy and safe like a womb.

"The light is warm and golden, and you can see that it flickers slightly on the wall of the tunnel. You round a curve in the tunnel and come out into a small chamber where a very old woman sits with her drum, playing a heartbeat rhythm. She wrinkles up in a smile and welcomes you, gesturing for you to be seated on one of the fat cushions that surround her.

"She has something to say to you. You lean in closely and she speaks . . . *(Pause for about a minute here.)*

"You thank her for her words of wisdom and give her a gift." (pause) "She is happy with what you have given her, and she leads you to the other side of the chamber where several tunnels lead up and away from her home. You choose a tunnel and begin to come back up, but then you see something on the ground and pick it up. What is it? *(Pause again while people examine the item.)*

"Keep this gift of the Earth always. When you come back, you may wish to draw a picture of it, or write it down in your journal. You continue up and feel a cool breeze on your face as you see a brighter light ahead of you. You emerge into this sacred circle, surrounded by all the others who have been to the old woman's chamber, and you come back into your body. When you are ready, slowly open your eyes, and be here now."

The drummer gradually fades the heartbeat away and allows the room to be silent. You and the directional priest/esses give out the food and drink, allowing people to sit in silence or discuss what they saw as they desire. After about five or ten minutes, stand in the center of the circle and say:

"Today we have experienced the ecstasy that drums can help us find inside ourselves, and we have experienced the primal heartbeat that a drum can represent. We have blessed our drums, and of course they have blessed us. May it ever be so, until the end of time. But now we must close our circle and bring our experiences home."

If the God and Goddess were called, dismiss them in the same manner as they were called. The elements are also dismissed using the same instruments that were used to call them, and the circle is opened. Say, "Merry meet, merry part, and merry meet again" or whatever ending is traditional for your group to indicate that the ritual is over.

Dumb Supper for the Ancestors

WHEN: Samhain

WHERE: Indoors

CAST: HP/S

MINIMUM NUMBER OF PARTICIPANTS: One

RITUAL DRESS: Your choice

SUGGESTED SONGS: "What Is Remembered Lives" by Reclaiming, "Breaths" by Sweet Honey in the Rock

PROPS: Plates, cups, utensils

ALTAR SETUP: One large main altar to contain all the food dishes, serving ware, etc., a large empty offering plate, your ritual necessities

CAKES AND ALE: The ritual itself provides the food and drink

NOTES: Make sure people understand that this is a potluck affair and that they are to bring dishes that their deceased loved ones enjoyed in life. Provide extra beverages since most people will probably bring food.

Perform basic housekeeping such as announcements and so on. Create your sacred space, call the elements/guardians, and call to your deities as you usually do. Make sure this is done carefully and well since your group will be calling up strong emotions and the memories of your beloved dead—you don't want any spirits following people home.

Have all participants place their food on the altar and talk about what they brought and why. Follow each person's statement with the simple one-line chant "What is remembered lives."

Now explain the next section of the ritual:

"We will be eating these foods as a dumb supper. If you're unfamiliar with a dumb supper, it's a simple ritual in which you sit down and eat with your beloved dead in silence, communing with them and remembering them. Since you are silent, and they sit with you in silence, it's been called a 'dumb' supper.

"As you gather your foods from the altar, add a bit to the communal offering plate so that your beloved dead can come and share this bounty with us. As you sit and eat their favorite foods, take your time . . . think of them, laugh, cry, and know that they are always with us in one form or another."

If desired, play some quiet "new age" gentle music in the background for a pleasant atmosphere. Allow plenty of time for everyone to finish eating and have a place for the dirty plates to go to keep the area neat. When all have finished, let people that would like to share their visions or messages speak for a time.

Sing or play the song "Listen," providing the words for everyone to take home, discussing them if the group would like to do this. If anyone senses lingering spirits that need to return to the other side of the Veil, these should be spoken to gently now.

Dismiss the elements and open the circle in the same ways that these were done at the beginning. Say, "Merry meet, merry part, and merry meet again" or whatever ending is traditional for your group to indicate that the ritual is over. ❧

Yule Dark Mother Goddess

WHEN: Yule

WHERE: Indoors

CAST: HP/S, Dark/Light Mother, four directional priest/esses, extras for dark/light spirits

MINIMUM NUMBER OF PARTICIPANTS: Six

RITUAL DRESS: All cast members wear black (see Notes below)

SUGGESTED SONGS: "Nightmare Before Christmas Overture" by Danny Elfman, "Air I Am" by Andreas Corbin, "Ancient Mother," "Heaven and Hell" by Vangelis, "Metamorphosis" by Diana Paxson

PROPS: Large cauldron, battery-operated holiday light string, wax paper, fresh greenery boughs, candle crown, conch shell horn, extra costumes (see below), extra candles of any kind, hand-made Yule ornaments to give away, several baskets to hold the ornaments

ALTAR SETUP: Four small altars, one in each direction (wooden TV trays are perfect for this), and a "central" working altar (can be off to one side as well). The East altar should have incense and a yellow candle. The South altar should have matches and a red candle. The West altar should have a bowl of water and a blue candle. The North altar should have a bowl of salt and a green candle. The "central" altar should have a black candle for the Dark Mother, a white candle for the Light Mother, and the usual tools and embellishments such as an athame, fresh greenery, and so on

CAKES AND ALE: White grape juice, honey cakes

NOTES: All cast members except the HP/S will need white robes that can be slipped quickly over the head at the time of transformation from dark to light, perhaps a simple poncho that can be tied with a white cord. Ideally, the Dark/Light Mother should have a reversible black/white cape with glittery stars painted on both sides. Also be sure there is an "offstage" area (hallway, stage curtain, adjacent room, etc.) where the spirits and the Dark/Light Mother can be concealed and do a short costume change. The cauldron is placed in the center of the hall, then the battery-powered lights are placed inside, then the wax paper to diffuse the light, then greenery around the edges to hide the edges of the wax paper and to add depth and beauty to the cauldron. Greenery can encircle the outside of the cauldron as well. The extra candles should be placed all over the hall for extra illumination.

After the five-minute warning chime, begin playing the "Nightmare Before Christmas Overture" quietly in the background. After the song is over, perform basic housekeeping such as announcements and so on. Next you will be doing a grounding of the group which also serves as a sort of explanation of the ritual:

"The winter solstice is the cusp . . . the moment that the darkness turns to light, that the sun is reborn for another year. Tonight we will be celebrating that transition, celebrating the duality and contrast of the dark and the light.

"Become comfortable and close your eyes. Relax your muscles . . . take a deep breath and relax even further . . . and take another deep breath, feeling the sacred Air fill you, purify you, heal you. As you breathe, become aware of your heartbeat . . . your blood . . . the warmth of you, a living creature of magic. Feel that warmth become the candle's flame . . . the sacred Fire of energy, of drive, of creation, and of destruction, too. Feel that Fire inside yourself . . . . Now relax and become aware of the sacred Waters of life within you . . . the saliva in your mouth, the liquid of your blood, the waters of your womb or of your seed. . . . Tears of salt water like the ocean, tears of joy and of sorrow, of hurt and of healing . . . feel the healing waters within you now . . . Now, as the waters lay upon the surface of the sacred Earth, feel the Earth below you . . . feel your body touch the floor, then the soil, then the deep, deep rock . . . Feel your own bones as the bones of the Earth . . . look deep within the Earth as you also look deep within yourself . . . you have the strength to do what must be done . . . to turn the Wheel once again.

"Feel all these things within *you* . . . feel that you are a perfect reflection of the elements. . . . Know this simple truth, feel this perfect balance, and become aware of the other perfect beings next to you . . . all around you . . . and be here now."

When it appears that everyone is "back," cense and asperge the circle and people, using an appropriate chant such as "Air I Am." The circle is cast as you normally would do this or in silence.

Beginning in the East, the East priest/ess lights the yellow candle and says:

"Spirits of the East, of wind and wing, of new beginnings and the dawn, we ask that you be here with us tonight and lend us your power as we turn the Wheel of the year once more. Hail and welcome."

The South priest/ess then lights the red candle, saying:

"Spirits of the South, of ferocious flame, of passion and the high, hot sun, we ask that you be here with us tonight and lend us your power as we burn away the old to help the new shine brightly. Hail, and welcome."

The West priest/ess lights the blue candle and says:

"Spirits of the West, of wave and foam, of healing and the sunset, we ask that you be here with us tonight and lend us your power as we wash away the hurt and bathe in new possibilities. Hail, and welcome."

Finally, the North priest/ess lights the green candle and says:

"Spirits of the North, of caves and secrets, of stability and the dark of night, we ask that you be here with us tonight and lend us your power as we find the balance, as we sleep with the deepness of the dead and then awake to find the sun shining through the trees. Hail, and welcome."

Those that are portraying dark spirits should move to the "offstage" area where Dark Mother will be waiting. They should be ready to enter by the end of the narration and when they hear the song "Ancient Mother" begin.

Give an introductory narration as the cast find their places offstage:

"The solstice celebration that we enjoy today has been touched by many cultures over the millennia. What began as a simple observance of the longest night and shortest day when the sun is least virile has become a celebration both somber and festive. Along the way, mysterious creatures of the dark as well as bright spirits of light have made themselves known to us. Before we turn the wheel once more, let us welcome and embrace the Dark Mother and meet some of these creatures of mystery . . . creatures of the midwinter darkness, when the sun is too weak to save you and death is never too far away."

Light the black candle on the central altar and say:

"Great Dark Mother, Crone of the crossroads, She who cuts the cord, we humbly ask for your attendance and help tonight as we turn the wheel, as we change the world, as we change ourselves. Help us understand the darkness within and without."

Begin to sing "Ancient Mother" and encourage the group to join in. The Dark Mother processes slowly into the hall, and the dark spirits variously follow, hide under her cape, and so on. She reaches the center of the room and stops. "Ancient Mother" comes around to its stopping point. Say:

"We welcome you, Dark Mother."

The Dark Mother replies:

"The Mother blesses her children".

Begin playing "Hell" by Vangelis or other "dark" music and dim the lights. As the Darkness narration is read, the dark spirits come out from behind the Dark Mother and harass the audience with taunts, ugly faces, and perhaps little pinches (you should be able to tell if this is okay with individuals if you know them—if you don't, leave out the pinching).

Read the Darkness narration as the music and cavorting are going on:

"To the Greeks, the Karkantzaroi [*car-cant-za-roy*] are a very real and living nuisance. They are half-animal, half-human monsters, with huge heads, glaring red eyes, goats' or asses' ears, blood-red tongues hanging out, ferocious tusks, monkeys' arms, and long curved nails. From dawn till sunset they hide themselves in dark places, but at night they issue forth and run wildly to and fro, rending and crushing those who cross their path. Destruction and waste, greed and lust mark their course. When a house is not prepared against their coming, by chimney and door alike they swarm in, and make havoc . . . they overturn and break all the furniture, befoul all the water and wine and food which remains, and leave the occupants half dead with fright or violence.

"In Sweden, trolls are believed to ride over the heaths on wolves, brooms, or shovels to their night assemblies, where they dance and drink and make merry under their stones. . . .

"From Iceland comes the legend of the gigantic Yule Cat, who eats lazy humans. Those who do not help with the work of their village to finish all work on the autumn wool by Yuletime not only miss out on the Yule reward of a new article of clothing, they may become sacrifices for the dreaded Yule Cat.

"In England the fairies cause mischief during the Yuletide season. For example, the pewter and brazen vessels had to be made so bright that the maids could use them as mirrors—otherwise the fairies would pinch them.

"Mother Berchta appears in Germany. She visits houses often, and if they are clean, she blesses the occupants, but if they're untidy, she curses the household with disease and scares the livestock. Everyone must leave food for Mother Berchta. If she is forgotten she will cut open the stomachs of the disrespectful, remove the food there and sew them up using a plowshare threaded with chains."

Now the Dark Mother speaks:

"Who will take my hand and follow me into the dark, to the center of the wheel? Meditate on what you wish to release, to transform. At the center, release it into the cauldron . . . it will take what you wish to be rid of and help you find a positive change to fill the void. As you approach the center of the wheel, you are approaching your own rebirth, the transition from dark to light, the place where all changes. Carry away with you the light of hope, the light of things to come in the new year, the light of change. Release that spark when the energy is high."

The music is changed to a song that's not quite dark and not quite light—best of all would be a song that shifts from a darker sound to ending on a lighter, happier note. You could also use a group of drummers that can quicken the pace at the end of the spiral dance. The Dark Mother takes the hands of the dark spirits, the last dark spirit takes the hand of someone in the crowd, and the spiral dance begins widdershins. You and any other cast members need to get to the center at this point so that they can help with the costume change (don't forget to bring them with you to the center, as well as the candle crown, matches, and conch-shell horn—put them all in a basket together to make this easier). When The Dark Mother and dark spirits are at the center, they quickly put on their white costumes and go back out to finish the dance. When the last person has reached the center, the Light Mother needs to quicken the pace to raise energy. She keeps the people moving quickly until you signal the energy release by blowing the conch-shell horn four times.

Cue or sing the song "Metamorphosis," or all can join in a song about transforming from darkness into light. Light Mother and spirits drop hands, then the Light Mother stands in the center as the spirits flow around her in order to light the candles in the crown. Those not helping with the crown need to go light the assorted extra candles around the perimeter of the room.

Pinch out the black candle and light the white one on the central altar, then say:

"Welcome, Lady of Light, you who bring forth the Spring, help us turn the wheel at this time of change. Help us create our futures."

The Light Mother responds:

"The Mother blesses her children."

You then say:

"We have planted the seed. . . . Now be blessed by the spirits of light."

The spirits take up the baskets of Yule ornaments, motion for people to return to their seats if necessary, then go to their quarters and allow people to take an ornament of their choice as they go around the circle.

Read the following narration (slowly to allow time for ornament distribution):

"Just as the world is not simply dark or light, neither are the spirits we have met tonight. Mother Berchta may seem terrifying, but she is also a fierce creator and protector of fertility and new life. In pre-Christian Germany, she is the white lady, beautiful Hulda the Benign who drives a carriage full of presents through villages where respect has been shown to her. When it snows, people believe she is making her bed and her quilt feathers are flying.

"The fairies that pinch the servants for not polishing the silver well enough may also leave a coin in their shoe for a job well done. You've probably also heard tales like the Shoemaker and the Elves where the little folk help out humankind rather than causing mischief. And we all know how the cat can be both ferocious and loving.

"Remember well the lessons of darkness and light and the shades in between. As we welcome the sun at solstice, do not forget that the sun casts shadows where the darkness dwells, and that the dark winter sky holds the stars that are the suns of other places. Dark, Light, death, life, day, night . . . these are but two sides of the same coin. Now that we have danced the wheel around a little closer to the spring, let us enjoy and be nourished by the gifts of the Earth."

The spirits now take up the pitchers of juice and plates of cakes for the crowd. Pass out cups and announce that anyone who wishes to seek the blessings of the Lady may approach her now. Play some quietly soothing and light music.

When people have finished their refreshments and have finished visiting the Lady, say:

"Thank you Lady, thank you for the gifts of the dark and the light. Please, leave us your light for another year and help us change ourselves and the world. Go if you must, stay if you will. Hail and farewell."

Light Mother acknowledges (nods, bows, whatever), then turns away from the crowd and kneels down where the candle crown is removed and she is covered with her white cloak. The lit crown is placed on the central altar. The elements are then dismissed, beginning in the North.

The North priest/ess holds aloft the green candle and says:

"Spirits of the North, of caves and secrets, of stability and the dark of night, we thank you for being here with us tonight and lending us your power. Go if you must, stay if you will. Hail and farewell."

The green candle is extinguished, then the West priest/ess holds aloft the blue candle, saying:

"Spirits of the West, of wave and foam, of healing and the sunset, we thank you for being here with us tonight and lending us your power. Go if you must, stay if you will. Hail and farewell."

The blue candle is extinguished, then the South priest/ess holds aloft the red candle, saying:

"Spirits of the South, of ferocious flame, of passion and the high, hot sun, we thank you for being here with us tonight and lending us your power. Go if you must, stay if you will. Hail and farewell."

The red candle is extinguished, then the East priest/ess holds aloft the yellow candle, saying:

"Spirits of the East, of wind and wing, of new beginnings and the dawn, we thank you for being here with us tonight and lending us your

power as we await the solstice dawn. Go if you must, stay if you will. Hail and farewell."

The yellow candle is extinguished and the circle is opened in the same manner that it was cast. Say, "Merry meet, merry part, and merry meet again" or whatever ending is traditional for your group to indicate that the ritual is over. ❧

The Burning Times

WHEN: Samhain

WHERE: Inside

CAST: HP/S (drummers are also good)

MINIMUM NUMBER OF PARTICIPANTS: One

RITUAL DRESS: Black

SUGGESTED SONGS: "Rise with the Fire" by Starhawk

PROPS: Black woman-shaped candle, large tray of sand, assorted dry woods and herbs (a few splinters of resinous "fatwood" is also recommended to get things burning well), image of Kali

ALTAR SETUP: One central altar large enough for the tray of sand, Kali image, and all your necessities

CAKES AND ALE: Homemade wheat bread, hot spiced apple cider

NOTES: Have people bring drums, etc., for energy raising.

Perform basic housekeeping such as announcements and so on. Welcome everyone with a short introduction:

"Tonight we will acknowledge loss, but not in the way you might think. Tonight we will also acknowledge rebirth in ourselves as Witches from the ancient magics that have always been in this world. We will mourn, and we will send energy to positive change. We will wail with grief, and we will change the world.

"Kali is important in Hindu belief not because she is a hideous killer with a necklace of severed heads and a bloody blade in her hand. Kali is the essence of what we will be doing tonight—she is death, yes, but she is the freeing of the spirit from its prison of flesh through the fires of change. Kali does not appear ferocious to harm us, she does this to attack our enemies instead.

"We will be taking our pain, our sacred rage, and transforming that energy into a powerful force for change in the world. Let us now begin this sacred working, for it's never too soon to change the world."

Cast the circle tightly, and call in the elements as you normally do. Now give a brief history of the Burning Times, building the pyre for the candle as you speak (lay several pieces of dry wood on the sand, then place the candle on top, then lay more wood and herbs around the bottom of the figure's feet):

"We all know about what is called the Burning Times, or the Inquisition, or the Witch Hunts of our past. Researchers now estimate the number killed at about ten thousand people, most of them simply people with valuable property, people with a physical deformity, too many skin blemishes, rheumatoid arthritis, or even cranky neighbors. People who had the misfortune of being in the wrong place at the wrong time. People with a black cat living in their barn, or a next-door neighbor whose cow had suddenly died. Midwives and healers who could not save a baby or its mother. Men who loved other men. Women who loved other women. People who had visions, even if they were sent by their Christian God. Wisefolk who knew the secrets of the plants, the stars, the elements, and the Old Ones. Anyone who acted contrary to what the church thought was proper. People like you and me.

"And so the church condemned them to death out of fear, or greed, or both. All across Europe, and into the colonies of America, the church tried these people and believed the accusing fingers. They were sentenced to die. They were sentenced to be hanged . . . or drowned . . . or tortured . . . or crushed . . . or beheaded . . . or burned alive. Their screams intermingled with their prayers as their flesh blackened, their hair rose into the terrible hot wind of the flames, then was burned away . . . then all was silent except the crackling of the pyre under them."

Silently light the candle and pyre, then say:

"Let us never forget! Let us mourn these poor souls because what is remembered lives! Let us taste our sacred rage on our tongues and let it escape from our lips as we scream to the heavens!"

Begin keening and wailing as the candle and pyre burn, encouraging everyone to join in with you. When the keening finally dies away and/or when you sense the energy is at a peak, say:

"Now let us direct this energy toward positive change! Let us whip it up, shape it, take it from the past and send it out as freedom, as magic, as the manifestation of the future we are creating right now, this moment!

Begin the "Fires of Freedom" chant and drumming to raise energy, then, when the energy is at its peak, throw up your arms, shout "Now!" and channel its release outward. Make sure everyone (including you) grounds and has a moment to collect themselves, then move on to the bread and cider. Allow several minutes for people to eat and

be nourished, both body and soul, then close the ritual:

"Can you feel it? Can you feel the change? Maybe it's just whispers in the air . . . maybe it's a tiny stirring under the earth . . . but we have done some powerful magic tonight. May our visions of how the future should be manifest in beauty and sacredness. May the world be a better place now that the Witches are back. So mote it be."

Now thank the elemental powers and open the circle in the same way that these things were done at the beginning. Say, "Merry meet, merry part, and merry meet again" or whatever ending is traditional for your group to indicate that the ritual is over. ❧

The Four Seasons

When: Yule
Where: Inside
Cast: HP/S, four seasons priest/esses
Minimum Number of Participants: Five
Ritual Dress: White or black for the HP/S,

seasonal colors and costumes for the four seasons priest/esses
Suggested Songs: "The Seasons" (traditional) as recorded by Loreena McKennitt, "Turn! Turn! Turn!" by Pete Seeger

PROPS: CD player, lyrics for everyone, "Wheel of the Year" wreath, little tied cloth bundles or pouches for everyone, containing lavender; a dried apple piece; grains of wheat; and a small stone (green agate, aventurine, quartz, snowflake obsidian, or another appropriate stone of your choice), a basket to hold the bundles

ALTAR SETUP: One main altar for the necessities, four smaller directional altars with seasonal colors and decorations

CAKES AND ALE: Gingerbread and tea

NOTES: To make a "Wheel of the Year" wreath, simply glue lots of seasonal floral items to a straw wreath base—use daffodils and other spring flowers, mushrooms, frogs, and birds for spring; roses, berries, and butterflies for summer; wheat, apples, nuts, oak leaves, grapes, and squirrels for autumn; pine branchlets, snowflakes, and other white or clear shimmery accents, dark eucalyptus leaves, and holly sprigs for winter.

Perform basic housekeeping such as announcements and so on. With the tool of your choice, cast the circle by saying:

> "As I walk around the circle, I walk around the wheel of the year. As we live within the wheel, may this place be blessed by all the seasons of the Earth and the gifts they bring."

Each of the four seasonal priest/esses stands by their direction's altar (East = Spring, South = Summer, West = Autumn, North = Winter) and calls to their element and season:

EAST/SPRING: "Hear me, guardians of the eastern realms! You, the spirits of new beginnings, where the sun is born each day . . . we ask that you come to us and lend us your power and protection. Hail, and welcome!"

SOUTH/SUMMER: "Hear me, guardians of the southern realms! You, the spirits of the fiery sun who stands tall at the summer solstice . . . we ask that you come to us and lend us your power and protection. Hail and welcome!"

WEST/AUTUMN: "Hear me, guardians of the western realms! You, the spirits of emotion, the joy of harvest and sadness of loss . . . we ask that you come to us and lend us your power and protection. Hail and welcome!"

NORTH/WINTER: "Hear me, guardians of the northern realms! You, the spirits of the silent snows, of deadly cold, of gray and white . . . we ask that you come to us and lend us your power and protection. Hail and welcome!"

Now give a brief introduction to the ritual:

> "Yes, we are in the time of gray and white . . . the clouded skies, the star-filled but frozen nights, the time to reflect on what we have nurtured this past year and what we will grow in the coming year. And as we reach the darkest

night, we know that the sun will rise again to strength, and we celebrate that spark of hope and that endless cycle of life on our planet.

"The Wheel of the Year is eternal. The Wheel teaches us many lessons, brings us many gifts, helps us grow. So let us now celebrate this endless cycle, this cosmic spiral dance through the years. Let us honor the Wheel of the Year."

Cue the music as the four priest/esses pick up their seasonal decorations from their individual altars, then line up in front of the main altar in order, beginning with East/Spring on the far left. On "Come cheer up your hearts and revive like the spring. . . ," Spring holds up his or her seasonal decorations and *slowly* walks deosil around the circle, returning to his or her original place before the main altar when the circle is completed. On "Don't you see the little lambs. . . ." Summer follows suit. On "Next cometh Autumn. . . ." Autumn follows suit. On "All nature seems too weary now. . . ." Winter follows suit. On "And so the world goes round and round . . ." the HP/S with the Wheel of the Year wreath goes around in the same way and ends the procession.

Have all the priest/esses return their items to their altars and say:

"What season is your favorite? I'm sure many of you do have a favorite, but for some, it may take more thought. When you're ready, speak

out the name of your favorite season and tell us why you love it. I'll go first . . ."

Speak the name of your favorite season and why. If people are slow to get started, have the seasonal priest/esses give their answers. When everyone has finished speaking, describe the next part of the ritual:

"Now we'll be lighting a candle up here at the main altar. This represents not only the newborn light of the solstice, but also a wish or a prayer for the coming year. If there's something you wish to manifest, or something you hope will happen, etc., then hold that in your mind as you come up, one by one, and light one of the candles."

Cue the song "Turn, Turn, Turn" and have it playing quietly in the background as people light their candles. When people have finished lighting their candles, take the basket of tied bundle gifts and call the four priest/esses to the main altar. Have them all bless the bundles with their energy as you say:

"These bundles contain gifts from the four seasons of the Earth. Lavender buds for fragrant Spring flowers, dried apple for Summer's fruits and the Summerland, wheat grains for Autumn's bounty, and a special stone for cold Winter's bones. Keep these as reminders of the gifts of the Earth and of the Wheel of the Year. If you like, you can keep the stone and return the other gifts to the Earth after a year and a day has passed."

Everyone is given a bundle, then the priest/esses bless the cakes and ale as the spirit moves them. Distribute the food to everyone with their help, then allow several minutes for people to enjoy it. When everyone has finished, move on to the final chant:

"As we sit on the cusp of the new year's dawn, let us sing to welcome back the light. The Wheel turns ever onward, so let us celebrate the year to come, a year full of hope, good things, and magic."

Lead the circle in "Light Is Returning," clapping in time and encouraging everyone else to do the same. When you sense the time is right, end the song and begin to close down the circle, starting in the North:

NORTH: "Hear me, guardians of the Northern realms! We thank you for coming to us and blessing us with your gifts and your power. Hail, and farewell."

WEST: "Hear me, guardians of the Western realms! We thank you for coming to us and blessing us with your gifts and your power. Hail, and farewell."

SOUTH: "Hear me, guardians of the Southern realms! We thank you for coming to us and blessing us with your gifts and your power. Hail, and farewell."

EAST: "Hear me, guardians of the Eastern realms! We thank you for coming to us and blessing us with your gifts and your power. Hail, and farewell."

Open the circle (deosil) by saying:

"As I walk around the circle, I walk around the Wheel of the Year. As we open this sacred space, may we go forth and walk in beauty throughout the blessed year to come. Hail to the new year!"

Say, "Merry meet, merry part, and merry meet again" or whatever ending is traditional for your group to indicate that the ritual is over.

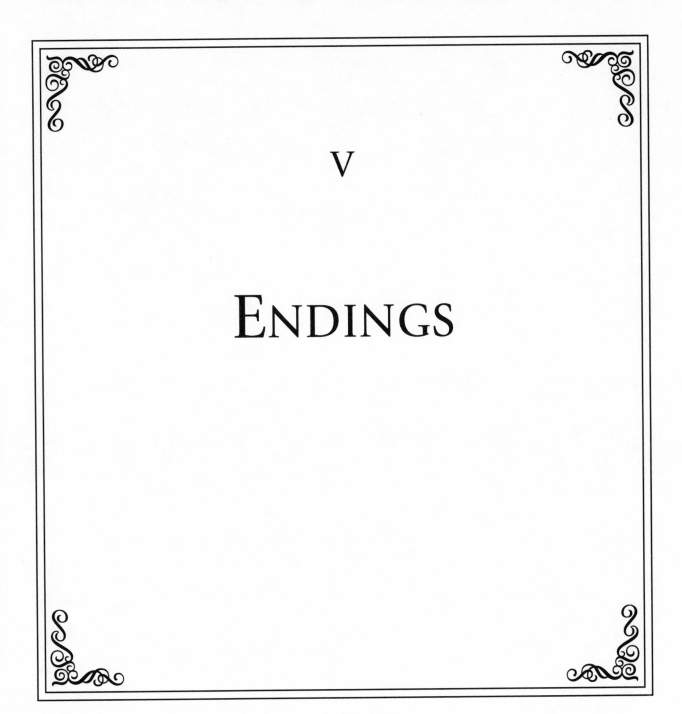

V

ENDINGS

Ending a Relationship

WHERE: Outside or inside

CAST: HP/S (you should be the opposite gender from the ex-partner if at all possible to avoid having emotions and/or anger accidentally transferred to you during the ritual)

MINIMUM NUMBER OF PARTICIPANTS: One

RITUAL DRESS: Your choice

SUGGESTED SONGS: "She Changes Everything She Touches" by Starhawk, "We Are the Changers" (author unknown), "Circle of Light" by Betsy Rose, "Everything Hurt Is Healed Again" by Starhawk, "Give Me a Little Sunshine" by Jill Schumacher (especially nice for an outside daytime ritual), "Dance Me into Life" or "Wisdom Path" by Cynthia R. Crossen

PROPS: Letter written in advance, small cauldron or metal dish with sand in the bottom, charcoal tablet, at least nine assorted skeins or balls of cotton yarn, scissors or a very sharp ritual knife, besom

ALTAR SETUP: One main altar with the necessities

CAKES AND ALE: Your choice

NOTES: This is also a good ritual for dealing with a partner's death if the person is having trouble letting go and wants a ritual to help with that. This can also be done by everyone in the group if a group member has left in a painful or chaotic way such that it needs resolution. Have the person who wishes to perform the ritual write a letter to his or her ex-partner prior to the ritual—it can say whatever the person wants and be as long as desired.

Perform basic housekeeping such as announcements and so on.

Cast the circle, call the elements, and call any deities as desired (if you're eclectic, Sekhmet and Kali are particularly good "severing" goddesses to call upon). Place a charcoal tab in the cauldron or dish and, after it has caught and is starting to burn, give a brief explanation of the ritual:

"We are here today to help [name] heal . . . she [or he] has just gone through a painful end to her [or his] relationship, and would like our help in severing all ties so that healing may begin. It has been said that it is far better to make a clean break of things than to let things linger. . . . The surgeon slices cleanly so that healing may begin quickly, rather than slowly and painfully tearing away the injury. So today we will be lending our energy to a clean break and a fresh start for [name]."

Bring out the cauldron or dish or let the person in question walk up to it, depending on circumstances and your ritual space layout. Have the person declare what the letter's intent is, whether it was written with kind thoughts or anger toward the ex-partner, and have him or her drop it into the cauldron.

Everyone holds hands and hums or chants, directing the energy up and out if the letter is intended to send kind thoughts to the ex, or send it down to be grounded and transformed if the letter is full of anger and things to be gotten rid of. You can use a common transformation chant such as "She Changes Everything She Touches" or "We Are the Changers," or try the longer song "Circle of Light" if anyone knows it or has the recording.

When the paper is burned completely and the person is ready to move on, get out the cotton yarn. Instruct the person how to choose the threads:

"Think now on what things brought you two together and what you shared during your relationship. Even if you're angry now, there were reasons why you originally got together. Focus on one thing and select a thread to represent that thing. Take the end in one hand and spread your arms wide to pull out a length, then cut it and put energy and memories into what it represents. Keep doing that as long as you want until you have selected a thread for each thing you shared in your relationship. Then you can weave or braid the strands together to represent your relationship. When you're done, I'll take one end, you take the other, and cut the strands in two."

When the weaving or braid has been completed and the person is ready, hold the strands taut as he or she cuts them. Burn the remains in the cauldron or dish and use a healing song such as "Everything Hurt Is Healed Again," "Give Me a Little Sunshine," "Dance Me into Life," or "Wisdom Path."

By now everyone will be ready for cakes and ale. This is also a good time to talk about things if the person or the group would like to. When everyone has finished, thank the deities and elements and open up the circle in the same manner that it was cast. Before adjourning, sweep the ritual area with a besom to be rid of any lingering negativity, grounding and returning it as you sweep. When this has been completed, say "Merry meet, merry part, and merry meet again" or whatever ending is traditional for your group to indicate that the ritual is over.

Miscarriage

WHERE: Inside

CAST: HP/S, woman who has miscarried, Crone, drummers (optional)

MINIMUM NUMBER OF PARTICIPANTS: Three

RITUAL DRESS: Black or your choice

SUGGESTED SONGS: "The River Is Flowing" by Diana Hildebrand-Hull, "Breaths" by Sweet Honey in the Rock, "We Are a Circle" by Rick Hamouris

PROPS: Cypress oil or another oil evocative of the Crone, song lyrics if needed

ALTAR SETUP: One main altar with the necessities

CAKES AND ALE: Your choice, something comforting like warm homemade bread and butter

NOTES: This is intended to be a smaller ritual for personal healing when someone has gone through a miscarriage, but it can also be used for other unexpected deaths or losses. If the gender of the fetus was known, you may choose to call either the Lord in his guise of Dying God and sacrifice, or call upon the Crone as scripted below. Have the woman who has miscarried bring small gifts for everyone as a giveaway, and have everyone bring a small gift (*not* baby things—this is not a shower!) for the woman in return.

Perform basic housekeeping such as announcements and so on.

Cense and asperge all present. Cast the circle and call the elements in the manner most familiar and comforting to the woman who has miscarried.

Call forth the priestess who will be aspecting the Crone and ask if she is ready. When she is ready, anoint her with the cypress oil and have her be seated.

Now call to the Crone, asking everyone's help and energy to invoke her:

"Lady of the crossroads . . . Hecate . . . Morrigan of the battlefield . . . Kali the defender . . . Sekhmet the scalpel . . . Dark Fate who cuts the cord of life . . . Cerridwen of the cauldron . . . we call to you! Goddess of death and rebirth, you of a thousand names, come to us . . . help us understand . . . enter now your servant that she may speak your words to us and comfort us . . . Great one of life and death, we call to you! Teach us your mysteries, we pray to you. Welcome, Lady."

Give your Crone time to fully handle the aspecting and become ready to continue with the ritual. When she is ready, have the woman who has miscarried ask the Crone why this has happened to her—let the tears flow as they may. Let the Crone answer as she wants, or she may say:

"Blessings to you, daughter. There is no easy answer to these things, for it is a hard situation for both of you. Perhaps the best answer is that it is simply the way of things. Painful things happen to everyone. We are all here to learn, and we are all here to teach. You have learned from the experience . . . the child's spirit has learned . . . it is simply the way things are.

"Perhaps he [or she] was not ready yet and changed his mind. Perhaps there was a birth defect that would have been far worse if he had been born instead of miscarried. Perhaps there was something you both needed to learn. Who can say? It only makes the pain worse to try and guess.

"What's done is done . . . it is what it is . . . now let go . . . let the spirit return to the source with love. The hardest thing a parent can do is to let go of their child . . . so we will help you. Come close, my child, and we will sing with you."

The Crone (or a designated singer) leads everyone in the song "The River Is Flowing" as long as needed. If you use drummers for this section, be careful not to make the song into a dirge! The tempo and the mood should be gentle, soft, contemplative, and comforting. Let it go on as long as necessary for the healing to happen.

When the Crone senses that the woman is ready to move on, she hugs the woman and blesses her in her own words. When both are ready, devoke the Crone from her priestess:

"Dark Lady, Crone of life and death . . . we thank you and honor you for coming to us. Thank you for helping us to understand your ways a little more. Thank you for giving us the comfort of the Goddess. We ask now that you release your priestess, for this work can be tiring and difficult. Your presence in our circle is welcome, however, should you wish to stay nearby. Hail and farewell, Great One."

All participants incline their heads to honor the Crone as she leaves the priestess, allowing time for the woman to recover a bit before moving on. When she is able to continue, move into the giveaway:

"[Name] will now have a giveaway as part of this ceremony, to symbolize the gift that she has lost. In return we will give her new gifts to help fill the void left behind and show her that we love her."

When the giveaway has concluded, lead everyone in the song "Breaths" (or use a designated singer) or simply play the song from the CD. If your group is familiar with the song, they can sing along, or they may close their eyes and meditate on the words.

By now the group will be ready for nourishing and grounding cakes and ale, so allow plenty of time to serve and enjoy this. You can also use this time to lighten up the mood by looking at each other's gifts, discussing parts of the ritual, and so on.

When cakes and ale are done, have the group hold hands and sing "We Are a Circle" to show support and kinship for the woman and each other. Sing as long as everyone wants to and do a group hug if the mood seems right.

Thank the elements and open the circle in the same way that these were done at the beginning of the ritual. Say, "Merry meet, merry part, and merry meet again" or whatever ending is traditional for your group to indicate that the ritual is over. ❧

Helping Someone to Die

WHERE: Inside

CAST: HP/S

MINIMUM NUMBER OF PARTICIPANTS: Two

RITUAL DRESS: Your choice

SUGGESTED SONGS: "Set Sail" by Starhawk and Mara June Quicklightening

PROPS: Shroud, either the person's preference if they have one or a length of white linen

ALTAR SETUP: One main altar with the necessities or, if the dying person would like to have altars surrounding him or her, one tool altar and four directional altars.

NOTES: This ritual is designed for the experienced priest/ess who is able to handle a ritual of this importance and intensity and not come apart at the seams. If at any time the dying person needs anything, your job is to facilitate that and make the passage easier, whether it means bringing the ritual to a screeching halt or quietly listening to the whispers of the dying as the ritual continues around you.

Let other participants know in advance that death can be a disturbing thing to witness—depending on his or her condition, the dying person may have involuntary movements and/or sounds, may vomit or eliminate, or there may be other circumstances that sensitive people might find unpleasant or frightening.

This ritual assumes that the death is taking place outside a hospital setting. If it is inside a hospital, you will need to substitute things like incense and candles as well as get the necessary permissions—see the "Hospital Healing" ritual on page 143 for more ideas and information. For additional song and chant ideas, readings, and much more information on this topic, please read *The Pagan Book of Living and Dying* and *Awakening Osiris* (see bibliography).

Purify and bless the shroud in advance before arriving at the ritual location, and keep it out of sight if you think it would stress the dying person to see it. Remember to provide food and drink in an adjacent room for those keeping vigil with you so that they can stay nourished and grounded as needed.

Perform basic housekeeping. Cense and asperge everyone present as well as the ritual area. Cast the circle tightly or otherwise anchor the ritual space well while still allowing a portal or membrane for the dying person's spirit to cross over. Call to the elements/guardians, and call to the deity or deities of the person's choice.

Give a brief explanation of the working to the person:

> "This is our gift to you . . . this is not for us other than our desire to help you because we want to . . . if at any time you need or want something, you have but to let us know. If you want water or foot rubs, they will be there for you . . . if you want the lights dimmed, or for us to stop singing, or to sing something different . . . it will be done. This is your time and we are here for you. Is there anything you need now or anything you wish to say?"

When the person has finished, have the participants join hands and send him or her peaceful energy, perhaps accompanied by humming or a simple chant, by brushing the hair, gently touching or massaging, and so on.

A wonderful reading from *Awakening Osiris*, the Egyptian Book of Coming Forth By Day (usually called the Book of the Dead) is "Column of Gold." This edited translation by Normandi Ellis is particularly beautiful and inspiring:

"Beside the well, the sycamore rises. Beside the well, bright cornflowers grow. Do they rise on their tender stalks by will, or does some force of love mold them, drive them up? In the seed lies the will to become, and the greater will gives form. The power of the green shoot parts the earth. The water in the well is nourishing.

"I rise. My spine is of bone, sinew, and flesh. The power of gods courses through me and makes of my backbone a column of gold. I am the flower on its stalk, the budding of sycamore branches. I am the pillar on which the balance of life is weighed. Oh! My heart beats with joy; my life is golden as the humming of bees.

"I live for a time and pass away, but the column of gold will stand. The powers of gods shape us. As the gods will, so grows the universe.

"I rise. I am a column of gold, eternal, at peace, in harmony."

Allow a few moments of silence, then lead the group in the song "Set Sail" through all its verses. Here is another edited reading from *Awakening Osiris*, or you can devise a meditation that takes the person toward the light, over the rainbow bridge, flying with the ravens, or however their tradition recognizes the passage of spirit. If the person passes in the middle of the reading or meditation, continue until it is finished, for their spirit will still hear you and be guided across. Change the gender if appropriate:

"There is a house built for me on the rocks above the river where the fragrance of sweet roots and flowers keeps me company. To reach it I walked through papyrus marshes, spikelets of flowers towering. I plowed blue fields of flax, wove flowers into robes, crushed seeds to make oil. I have been many men in my passage, and as often as I thought of death, I thought of my garden.

"In the house there is food for the hungry. There is truth for those who can hear. At night, around the house, lie a thousand stars. The world's infinite arms carry the weary home.

"My bread is made of white corn. My beer is made of red barley. Hungrily I eat the gods' food and join a feast of mystery. Beneath fruit trees I ponder blossoms and tassels. Like the slender arms of dancing women are their hanging branches. I lie on my back and rejoice that it is not some vaporous dream. It is good to be here, a husband of earth.

"No greater joy exists than a walk among gardens, smelling herbs and flowers. I am lifted from the fretful earth as the green plant lifts clods of dirt. The sun pours its grace upon my head, its luster an oil falling from a red jar. This is the house where spirit was born. My bones and skin I leave like rags. I tear the veil and see the light I am. I feast on the silence of gods and the reticence of the world. Like smoke, like prayers, I am lifted up. Beauty is. All things are possible.

"Across the sky, gods and goddesses pass. Fire and air, spirit and light. What we imagine comes to pass. Thought finds its form. All forgotten things return. This moment marks a time. I endure the ages. My heart contains all I am, all flood of love, all thoughts invisible and vital as air.

"I leave the fields and enter the house. The journey ends there. I am a man returning home. Welcomed by family, embraced by ancestors, I am again that which I was, a soul, a fire clothed in heaven, a sparrow. Born of stars, I am a spirit naming the life that was always mine.

"Long tables are stacked with cakes. The scent of sandalwood rises. The house fills with birds and the smell of beer and ale. I enter the circle of sun. I speak with priests and hermits. I know words that draw light into the darkness. I know the vulture and the carcass. I know the eggs in the nest. I am a silver star hanging above the world, courage in the blackest night. I am swift water running, a lowing cow, the thought of myself in my father's forehead.

"I stand in peace before the world. I nourish and am nourished by love. Like a lotus, quiet upon the water, I listen and repeat the silence."

Allow the room to be silent for a time and, when you sense the moment is right, begin very quietly singing an appropriate song or chant. As you continue to keep vigil, sing other songs or chants as you feel the time calls for them.

When the person has passed over, cover his or her body and thank the deities, elements, and open the circle or sacred space when you're sure the spirit has found its way across. If it feels more appropriate to do so, you can leave the circle in place until a later time so that the body is protected. ❧

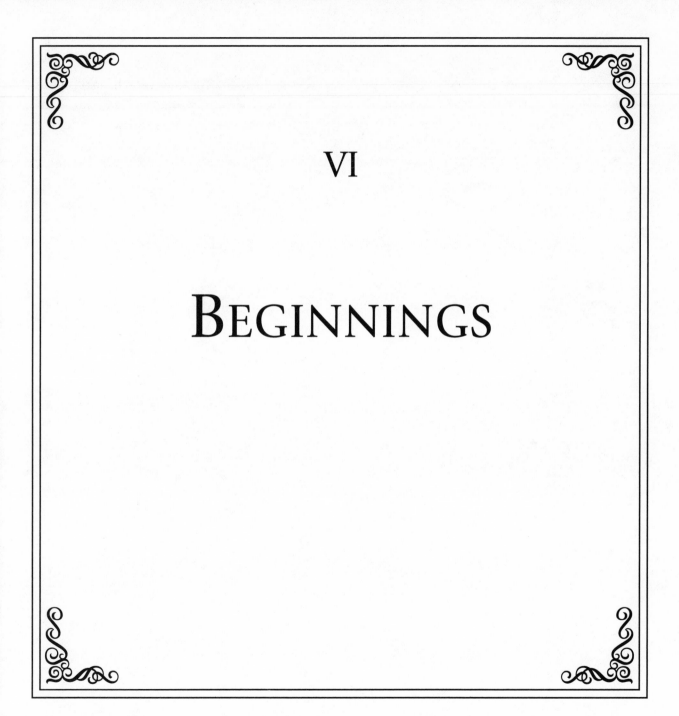

VI

BEGINNINGS

Coming of Age for a Boy

WHEN: It can be difficult to determine when a boy is ready to become a man. Two good indicators are the voice change and "wet dreams," or you can choose his thirteenth birthday. Begin the first half of the ritual in the evening and conclude it the next morning.

WHERE: Outside

CAST: HP, boy going through the rite

MINIMUM NUMBER OF PARTICIPANTS: Two

RITUAL DRESS: Your choice, the boy should wear ritual robes he has made himself

PROPS: Secluded men's lodge if no rural outdoor location is available for the overnight trial, supplies for this location (see below), protective amulet for the boy to wear (a tiger-eye stone, wrapped arrowhead, holed stone, crystal, or other stone pendant is good for this), fragrant herbs for strewing on the ground, red or green body paint, antlered circlet or headdress of real antlers, gifts (the HP should give an athame, God jewelry, staff, or other gift to signify his new manhood)

ALTAR SETUP: One main altar with the necessities

CAKES AND ALE: A large, hearty potluck feast

NOTES: Ideally, only men should be present for this ritual. Have everyone bring a "manhood" gift. This is a two-part ritual wherein the boy is sent off for his all-night trial and then returns the next day to finalize the rite. Before the first day's ritual the boy must bathe and dress in his new ritual robes that he has made himself. The trial site, which should be about ten miles from the ritual circle, should be shown to him in advance (with a map if necessary) so that he can navigate his way to the location himself. Prepare it by marking the site with flags (perhaps strips of cloth tied to branches if there are trees nearby) and setting it up as sacred space. He must pack with him any blankets needed, water, a flashlight, ritual items needed, and any basic needs such as medications.

Part 1: Perform basic housekeeping such as announcements and so on. Briefly describe the working to be done over the next two days:

"Brothers, we are here to bring a new member into our circle. He has so far proven to be worthy of the title "man," but he has one final trial before that can be declared before the gods. It is a path he must walk alone. He must learn what it means to rely on his own strengths as a man . . . to provide for himself and for others . . . to be strong in the face of fear. We will create this sacred space and hold it firm while [name] journeys on his own. [Name], are you ready to begin your trial?"

Presuming the answer is in the affirmative, continue the ritual by creating your sacred space as your group or tradition dictates, which can include purifying the area, casting the circle, and calling to the Lady and Lord. When you call the elements, call on them to teach and watch over the boy on his journey in particular, using wording such as:

"Mighty powers of the East, place where the Sun King is born each day, winged ones with sharp eyes, guard and guide [name] on his journey into manhood now and always. Hail and welcome.

"Mighty powers of the South, fires of freedom and strength, height of the sun's power, clever creatures of the desert sands, guard and guide [name] on his journey into manhood now and always. Hail and welcome.

"Mighty powers of the West, great sea storms and waterfalls, gentle rains and tears, place where the Sun King lays down his sacrifice, swimmers under the waves, guard and guide [name] on his journey into manhood now and always. Hail and welcome.

"Mighty powers of the North, place where the Old Ones lay buried, earthquakes and volcanos, mysteries of silence, bones of the Earth, four-leggeds of strength and endurance, guard and guide [name] on his journey into manhood now and always. Hail and welcome."

Call the boy forth and place the protective amulet around his neck. Tell him the details of the trial:

"Little brother, to be a man requires strength—strength of will, strength of body, and strength of mind. You are to travel to the location revealed to you alone, unassisted, and you are to camp there overnight. Make it a sacred space and pray for visions. Leave offerings. Be silent and listen. Record what you dream while you are there. This is a ritual of change—let it change you into a man. Take now what you need and go with our blessings. Come back as you are ready, but not before sunrise. Blessed be."

You may choose to drum or sing as the boy departs. When he has gone, prepare the ritual area for the next morning by strewing fragrant herbs on the ground.

Part 2: Just before sunrise, have a guardian sit out by the circle and watch for the boy's return. When the boy approaches, the guardian signals the other men to come into the ritual area and blocks his way into the circle. The guardian challenges him with something like "Who comes to this men's lodge? Why do you seek to enter?" When the answers are received to your satisfaction, the boy is admitted through the gate to the cheers, drumming, etc., of his new peers.

The new man is purified with either salt water or spring water poured over him. His face is painted with red or green body paint to signify his virility and transformation, and he is crowned with an antler circlet or headdress of real antlers.

Ask if he has a new name that he would like used in his community and if so, use it for the remainder of the ritual and feast. Anoint and bless him, then introduce him to the group. Say, "Welcome to the Brotherhood of Men" or similar wording as all clap, cheer, and embrace the new man. Give him your special gift.

Conclude the ritual by thanking the elements, opening the circle, and so on in the same manner that they were done the previous evening.

Say, "Merry meet, merry part, and merry meet again" or whatever ending is traditional for your group to indicate that the ritual is over and move to the feasting area for the potluck and gift-giving.

Coming of Age for a Girl

WHEN: Full moon or new moon immediately following the girl's first menses, whichever is more appropriate for your tradition—begin the first half of the ritual in the evening and conclude it the next morning.

WHERE: Outside

CAST: HPS, girl going through the rite, Watcher (can be HPS)

MINIMUM NUMBER OF PARTICIPANTS: Two

RITUAL DRESS: Your choice, the girl should wear robes she has made herself, the Watcher should have black, white, or red robes with a hood or scarf that covers her face

PROPS: Secluded women's hut if no rural outdoor location is available for the overnight trial, supplies for this location (see below), red body paint or henna, decorated hoop or gate of some kind for the girl to pass through on the second day, a red blanket or rug, flower petals for strewing on the ground, gifts (the HPS should give her a crescent moon circlet, sacred symbol necklace, red pouch containing bloodstone, red cingulum, or other gift to signify her new womanhood)

ALTAR SETUP: One main altar with the necessities

CAKES AND ALE: Feast that includes red foods like cherry juice, strawberries, etc.

NOTES: Ideally, only women should be present for this ritual. Have everyone bring a "womanhood" gift. This is a two-part ritual wherein the girl is sent off for her all-night trial and then returns the next day to finalize the rite. Before the first day's ritual the girl must bathe and dress in her new ritual robes that she has made herself. The site, if prearranged, should have waiting for her a red blanket (and/or other blankets/rain gear as needed for the weather), water, a musical instrument if desired, ritual supplies, and any supplies for physical needs such as medications. A flashlight should not be included—in the case of emergency, there will be an adult nearby because the Watcher will secretly keep vigil nearby to be sure she doesn't fall asleep (bring binoculars). If she will be choosing her own location, she will need to pack everything in and out herself.

Part 1: Perform basic housekeeping such as announcements and so on. Briefly describe the working to be done over the next two days:

"Women, we are charged with a sacred rite. We are guiding [name] on a path that we have all traveled in one way or another . . . the path to womanhood. We will create this sacred space and hold it firm while [name] journeys and keeps vigil with her sister moon. [Name], are you ready to begin the journey into womanhood?"

Presuming the answer is in the affirmative, continue the ritual by creating your sacred space as your group or tradition dictates, which can include purifying the area, casting the circle, and calling to the Lady and Lord. When you call the elements, call on them to teach and watch over the girl on her journey in particular, using wording such as:

"Spirits of the East, you of new beginnings and the winds of change, guide and guard [name] as she begins this trial and thus begins a new phase of her life. Hail and welcome!

"Spirits of the South, the fires of will and passion are yours. Guide and guard [name] as she enters this trial and learns the mysteries of women's blood. Hail and welcome!

"Spirits of the West, your waters are never still and reflect our emotions as they ebb and flow. Guide and guard [name] as she moves through this trial and explores the new emotions that her maturing body creates. Hail and welcome!

"Spirits of the North, all the mysteries of the earth are yours. Your dark caves are the Mother's womb, your red earth is her living flesh and blood. Guide and guard [name] as she completes this trial upon your soil. Hail and welcome!"

Call the girl forth and carefully draw a red crescent on her forehead in either body paint or henna. Tell her the details of the trial:

"Little sister, you are to go out and be alone until the morning. When you find your place, make it sacred. You are to remain awake all night in vigil with the moon, learning her mysteries, the mysteries of the monthly cycle of blood, the mysteries of magic that belong to women alone. You will have plenty of time to reflect on these things. Time to be silent and listen. Time to create new things. Time to grow into a woman.

"While you are awake holding vigil, your task will be to create a moon magic spell or ritual for whatever purpose you desire. I will privately hear your ritual tomorrow after you've rested. Take now what you need and go with our blessings and that of the Lady. Come back as you are ready, but not before sunrise. Blessed be."

You may choose to drum or sing as the girl departs. If she is choosing her own location, have someone watch where she goes. After darkness has fallen but before it's so late that she may fall asleep, the Watcher silently goes to a location close enough to the girl to watch her with binoculars but far away enough so as not to be detected. If at any time the girl does fall asleep, the Watcher must go wake her and say "Sister, remember your purpose" or similar wording.

The ritual area at the "home base" needs to be prepared for the girl's return in the morning, including the red blanket or rug to be knelt on and strewn flower petals.

Part 2: When it begins to get light, just before sunrise, the Watcher makes a final assessment of the girl's readiness and secretly returns to the ritual area when it looks as though the girl is ready to leave. The Watcher notifies the other participants that the girl is returning and changes into her other ritual clothes if necessary.

When the girl approaches, the decorated hoop or gate should be ready and have a guardian before it who blocks her way. The guardian challenges her with something like "Who comes to this circle of women? Why do you seek to enter?" When the answers are received to your satisfaction, the girl is admitted through the gate to the cheers, drumming, etc., of her new peers.

The new woman is purified with water, either poured over her or sprinkled gently. This can be salt water or clear spring water. Next, she kneels in the center of the circle on the red blanket or rug as corn pollen, cattail pollen, corn meal, or another sacred substance that demonstrates fertility is sprinkled over her. This can be in silence, accompanied by drums, or the other women can sing—there are many songs in the books *Songs for Earthlings* and *Circle of Song* that are wonderful for this.

Ask if she has a new name that she would like used in her community; if so, use it for the remainder of the ritual. Anoint and bless her, then give her your special gift (circlet, necklace, etc.). Introduce her to the group. Say, "Welcome to the Sisterhood of Women" or similar wording as all give her a group hug.

Serve the cakes and ale as everyone else gives her their gifts, then conclude the ritual by thanking the elements, opening the circle, and so on in the same manner that they were done the previous evening. Say, "Merry meet, merry part, and merry meet again" or whatever ending is traditional for your group to indicate that the ritual is over, then allow the new woman to exit and get some sleep if desired.

Eldership

WHERE: Inside or outside

CAST: HP/S, elder-to-be, drummer (optional)

MINIMUM NUMBER OF PARTICIPANTS: Two

RITUAL DRESS: Your choice

PROPS: White, red, and black candles and holders; if male, white, green, and brown candles and holders, shallow bowl of water, small pitcher or carafe of olive oil

ALTAR SETUP: One main altar set in the North with the necessities, the three (or six) candles, and the bowl of water and oil

CAKES AND ALE: Your choice or something improved with age like wine, cheese, and sourdough bread

NOTES: Have the person or people who will be honored set a goal in advance that they will demonstrate at the ritual, such as creating something, writing a poem, losing weight, learning a difficult song, taking a Kabbalah class, and so on. Have everyone else who will be present bring a gift for the elder(s).

Perform basic housekeeping such as announcements and so on. Cast the circle, call to the elements, and call to the Sage and Crone rather than the Lord and Lady.

Now discuss the purpose of the ritual and what eldership means to the group:

"Everyone . . . as you know we are here to bestow a special status upon [name] for his [or her] wisdom, achievements, and knowledge. It's not easy to let go of youth, especially in today's society, but all things change. It is the way of the Wheel, the spiral dance of life. It is our way.

"As Witches, we recognize the value of age, for it is only with age that some things can be learned and understood. We don't become disposable "old farts". . . we become respected Elders . . . Teachers . . . Crones and Sages . . . they have knowledge that only those in the autumn and the winter can understand. They hold the mysteries of life and death. The Crone stands at the crossroads. The Sage holds the lantern.

"Let's go around the circle now and say what we think an Elder is, what it means . . . how Elders benefit our community. I've already spoken long enough, so let's go to my left. . . ."

Allow everyone to say what they think, then move on to the meditation, which is only for the elders. You can have someone drum a single beat for the meditation, about one beat per second or even slower.

"[Name], close your eyes. You will now embark on the journey of transformation into Eldership. Breathe deep . . . feel your body relax . . . feel the darkness of night around you . . . and you begin to walk out into the darkness.

"You feel fir needles brush your body as you walk, the scent of the forest all around you . . . you hear the crunch of dry oak leaves on the ground under you . . . and you see, far off in the distance, a point of light. It's bright yellow and it flickers and moves a little. You continue walking. *(pause)*

"As you continue, you come out of the forest and find that your feet are upon a narrow dirt road. The dim starlight mingles with the yellow light ahead of you and you see two figures. Where they stand, you see a road coming in to meet the one you're on, making a triple crossroad. As you walk closer still, the two figures turn to greet you. You see an old woman, her face hidden under a black cloak, and an old man from whose tall staff a lantern hangs, illuminating the ground where the crossroads meet.

"The old woman pulls back her hood, and her face is your face. You look closely at the old man in the lantern light, and his face is your face. They smile and say something to you. *(pause—about a minute)*

"They acknowledge that your gift to them is your new status of Elder. You have joined their society, their clan, their path is now your path. They will teach you the secrets . . . the hidden mysteries . . . for you have the time and the will now to learn. You move more slowly these days, which is just what is needed to learn these things.

"The Crone looking into your eyes says "Thou Art Goddess" and kisses you on the cheek. The Sage looks in your eyes and says "Thou Art God" and kisses you on the other cheek. They each press something into your hand. If you don't know what it is right away, you will discover its purpose later. You look back up from your hand and they are gone, but now you hold the lantern staff, your face hidden inside a deep hooded cloak. *(pause)*

"The sky begins to brighten, but instead of illuminating the road as you would expect, it grows harder to see . . . the staff dissolves from your hand . . . the hood is pushed back from your face . . . and you find yourself looking at the forest around you in the gathering sunrise light . . . the bare branches of the oaks and maples revealing the true shape of the tree . . . a trace of frost outlining every leaf on the ground and every pine needle . . . The autumn and winter reveal their secrets in a quiet and subtle way. And you know how to see them now.

"The sky grows brighter still, almost too bright, and you breathe deeply as you prepare to return to the circle . . . bringing with you your gifts, your discoveries, and your new status as Elder with the blessings of the Lord and Lady. Breathe deeply again, and feel your body around you, the body of an Elder, shaped by years of wisdom and experience. When you are ready, open your eyes into your new existence, Elder [name]."

Anoint the Elder and say "You are Blessed" and/or other words of your choice as they come to you. Now say:

"One of the realms of the Crone or Sage is scrying and divination. You are able to see as only someone in your phase of life can see. You have just been with the Crone and the Sage and partaken of their power. Will you honor us now by pouring a bit of this oil upon the water so that you and we may scry?"

Have him or her come over to the main altar and drizzle a little of the oil into the bowl of water so that he or she may scry into it. Then have each person come up and scry into the bowl. This should be done silently and should not be shared unless someone wants to share what they have seen.

Next, have the Elder make a declaration of what they will do differently now that they are a Crone or Sage. Follow this up with the demonstration of the achievement of their goal (singing a song, reading their poem, and so on). Move on to cakes and ale and gift-giving and merriment!

Thank the deities, thank the elements, and open the circle in the same manner that it was cast. Say, "Merry meet, merry part, and merry meet again" or whatever ending is traditional for your group to indicate that the ritual is over. 🌿

Great Mother Initiation

WHERE: Where your group usually meets

CAST: HPS, everyone in the group

MINIMUM NUMBER OF PARTICIPANTS: Two

RITUAL DRESS: Your choice

SUGGESTED SONGS: "Ancient Mother" (traditional), "By a Woman" (unknown) or "We All Come from the Goddess" by Z. Budapest

PROPS: Oil to anoint the initiate, any group symbols or tokens that you wish to give the new initiate

ALTAR SETUP: One central main altar with the necessities plus a candle for each member of the group including the new initiate

CAKES AND ALE: Your choice (birthday cake might be a fun choice)

NOTES: This should be performed by a women's group (for obvious reasons) and is intended for groups that have no established or traditional initiation ceremony. If she is expected to, tell the initiate that she will need to discover her craft name and be prepared to present it to the group upon her initiation.

Perform basic housekeeping such as announcements and so on. Cast the circle, call the elements, and call to your group's deity or deities as you usually do this.

Explain a bit about what you will be doing (or do this in advance when the initiate is not there if you wish it to remain unknown):

"Today each of us, no matter how young or old, will represent the Great Mother for [name] and give her birth into this group. You can make it easy or difficult for her to pass through, offer her blessings as she passes . . . it's up to you. We will all stand in a circle and face left, allowing [name] to crawl through the tunnel formed by our legs and be birthed into the group. If you are unable to do this, you may arch your arms over her instead. First, let us call to the Great Mother, that she may hear us and be with us."

Have the initiate stand off to one side, outside the circle of the group, at the place where she will enter. Lead the rest of the group in the song "Ancient Mother," letting it flow and ebb as the group wishes. At least one loud swell in the music should be facilitated by you if the group seems overly quiet. During this song, each woman should light a candle on the altar to represent her-self—one candle should remain unlit to represent the new member yet to enter the circle.

Turn to the initiate and challenge her, asking why she wishes to be in your group, what she has to give, how she enters, and/or other questions. When her answers are to your satisfaction, say to the initiate "You are about to begin a new part of your life and be born into this group as a sister. This is your final challenge . . . to birth yourself. We hold the energy of the Great Mother within us . . . now it's up to you to pass through all of us and receive Her blessings."

Turn your back to her, face left, and stand with your legs apart, indicating that the rest are to do the same. Lead the circle in "By a Woman" or "We All Come from the Goddess" as the initiate crawls through the birth tunnel formed by your legs.

When she makes it through and comes out where she began, help your new sister to stand and embrace her. If it will be a part of your ritual, ask if she has decided on her craft/magical name and have her say it out loud to the group.

Face each other and anoint her forehead with a little dot of oil, saying, "Blessed be your mind, that you may always use your intelligence to make good decisions and be blessed with visions from the Goddess." Anoint her throat and say, "Blessed be your voice, that it may rise up singing in beauty and speak the holy words of the Goddess." Anoint her chest and say, "Blessed be your heart, that you may feel the love of the Goddess and give it to others in return." Anoint her womb and say, "Blessed be your womb, the source of all life, the cauldron of eternity, for thou art Goddess." Anoint her feet and say, "Blessed be your feet that have carried you here to us, and that will take you far-ther still on the path to enlightenment." Stand and say to her, "You are blessed by the Goddess."

Turn to the group and present the new initiate, using her craft name if she has chosen one, saying something like "I present to you [name], anointed of the Goddess, sister to us all." Have her light the last candle on the altar.

If the group is giving her gifts, have each person go up and give the new initiate their gift to her. When everyone else is done, give her the symbols or tokens of your group, such as a cord, piece of jewelry, and so on. Share cakes and ale, which can also be done at the same time as the gifting.

When everyone has finished, thank the Great Mother for Her presence and help in your own words. Thank the elements and open the circle as your group usually does this. Say, "Merry meet, merry part, and merry meet again" or whatever ending is traditional for your group to indicate that the ritual is over.

Founding a Group

WHERE: Outside or Inside

CAST: Everyone in the group

MINIMUM NUMBER OF PARTICIPANTS: Three

RITUAL DRESS: Your choice

SUGGESTED SONGS: "We Sing with Mother Earth," "We Are a Circle Within a Circle" by Rick Hamouris

PROPS: Tealight candles for everyone, a large tray or dish of sand to hold the lit tealights, yarn/string/cord long enough for the working, scissors, more yarn in the group's special or preferred color(s)

ALTAR SETUP: One central altar with the necessities

CAKES AND ALE: Your choice

NOTES: This ritual is intended for the official formation of a coven/circle/group that does not already have a traditional ritual for this occasion. Everyone who is to be a permanent member of this group must be present at this founding ritual. The ritual should ideally be performed where the group meets most often—the "home base" location.

Perform basic housekeeping such as announcements and so on. Cense and asperge everyone present, then cast the circle and call the directions/

Even number of people

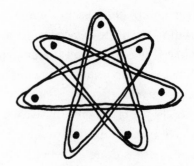

Odd number of people

elements/guardians as your group traditionally does this. Also call to your group's deities in the manner you usually do this.

When everything is set up the right way for you, state your group's purpose for existing. This can be previously written out, or each member can proclaim what they believe the group's function to be. End with "So Mote It Be" or whatever "Amen" sort of affirmation your group uses.

Now let each member take a tealight from the altar and speak about what the group means to them, what they bring to the group, what they get from the group, and why they want it to exist. Have them light the candle and place it back on the altar. Continue until everyone has had a chance to speak and light a candle.

Lead everyone in the zipper song "We Sing with Mother Earth," starting with you as an example of how to "zip" the name of the person into the song and so they can get the melody. Go around the

circle deosil, "zipping" each person's name into the blessing song.

Have everyone stand up, then take the special string and, walking to the outside of the circle, put it around each member's waist, starting with the person to your left and ending with yourself. If your group has an even number, loop the yarn around them; if your group has an odd number, make a star shape (see diagram).

Lead everyone in the chant "We Are a Circle Within a Circle," raising energy and putting it into the cord that binds you all together as a group. When the song is done (you'll sense when that is), pass the scissors around to each person and have them cut off a length of string to keep.

Using this string, plus more yarn/cord/string to equal three lengths that are about twenty feet long, have people pair off and begin twisting the ends of the string in opposite directions. When it is tightly twisted, have a third person hold it in the middle as the two people walk toward each other, still holding the string taut. The third person gently and carefully releases the middle while guiding the twisting cord until a neat rope has been made. Tie a knot about 3" up from each end and one cord is completed. It's a fun activity that has members work together to create cords unique to this group that will be used at future meetings.

When everyone has made a cord, put them on and raise energy to further link each other together as a group. You can raise energy however your group wishes to do this. Ground the energy to finally seal the group together.

Celebrate your newly founded group with cakes and ale in a relaxed atmosphere, but be careful not to let it go on too long or let it degenerate into chitchat and smoking breaks.

When people have finished eating and drinking and making merry, have everyone stand and hold hands. Give a brief statement about your wishes for the group, or let everyone say a few words, or otherwise comment on how the group has now been founded and its bright future and purpose. A group hug around the central altar is an excellent way to conclude the ritual before dismissing the elements and deities and opening the circle.

Say, "Merry meet, merry part, and merry meet again" or whatever ending is traditional for your group to indicate that the ritual is over.

Simple Handfasting

WHERE: Outside if possible

CAST: HP/S

MINIMUM NUMBER OF PARTICIPANTS: Three

RITUAL DRESS: Your choice

PROPS: Have the couple make a braided cord in advance from cotton yarn or embroidery floss—use red, plus a color of each person's choice, make all the strands as long as the shorter person or nine feet (your preference or theirs), an anointing oil for the witness(es) that promotes insight and honesty

ALTAR SETUP: One large main altar with the necessities, cord, gifts, etc.

CAKES AND ALE: Spice cake and sparkling cider

Notes: This is intended to be a smaller "year-and-a-day" handfasting ceremony rather than a full-blown legal wedding, although the ritual could be added to and enlarged for this purpose if desired.

Perform basic housekeeping such as announcements and so on.

Purify the ritual area and cast the circle as desired with the couple outside—you should be the only one inside the sacred space. Make a portal in this circle/sacred space for people to enter. Ideally this would have already been marked as a path with stones on either side, or a gateway with torches on either side, or a beaded curtain . . . whatever you want to use (or simply indicate it by standing at the edge where you want them to enter).

Call the couple over and challenge them to enter by saying "Why do you come into this sacred space today?" or something similar. Assuming they give a worthy answer, asperge each person with salt water and admit them to the circle, having them. Now call over any witnesses and guests and challenge them in the same way. Asperge everyone with salt water as they enter, and indicate that they are to be seated.

Call to the elements and Lord and Lady (or whatever deity/deities you prefer) to sanctify the joining of the couple and to bear witness. Do this with the wording that works best for you and the couple.

If there are official witnesses, call them forward. Anoint their ears and eyelids (*tiny* dot here!), telling them that they are witnessing a sacred union, so listen and watch carefully (or similar words of your choice). They may now stand by the couple or be seated again, your choice.

Ask the couple why they have come today and why they wish to be joined. Then ask who they honor in Spirit—who they wish to appear before to witness their vows. When they have finished answering, take the cord they made and ask them to join their hands. Wrap the cord around their hands, joining them together, and place your stronger hand on top of their hands. Say the following (or something similar of your own wording):

"By [deities they named], may these two people be united in love for a year and a day. Their hands are tied fast . . . thus they are handfasted together in the Old Way. If they do not wish to continue their relationship after the year and a day, they will no longer be bound. May they use this time to get to know each other better in all ways of life . . . may [repeat deities] bless them with love. So Mote It Be."

Unwrap their hands and give them the cord. Ask them to search within the circle and each find something from nature that they may keep on their altar or otherwise in a prominent place to remind them of their handfasting commitment to each other. Have them place these objects on the altar for the rest of the ritual.

Serve the cakes and ale, having the couple feed each other. During this period the couple also give each other the gifts they brought.

Close the ritual by thanking the deities you called, the elemental guardians/spirits, and open the circle in the same way it was cast. Say, "Merry meet, merry part, and merry meet again" or whatever ending is traditional for your group to indicate that the ritual is over.

Permanent Temple Consecration

WHERE: Wherever your permanent temple is to be kept

CAST: Everyone in the group

MINIMUM NUMBER OF PARTICIPANTS: Three

RITUAL DRESS: Your choice

PROPS: Statement of purpose (optional), small items to bury at the four corners of the space (shells, medallions, deity images, charms, etc.) and a trowel or items to hang on the walls in the four directions (posters, wreaths, banners, etc.)

ALTAR SETUP: One main altar with the necessaries

CAKES AND ALE: Your choice

NOTES: This ritual is intended for the consecration of a permanent temple/sacred space for groups that don't already have a traditional ritual for this occasion. Everyone who is a permanent member of the group must be present at this ritual.

Perform basic housekeeping such as announcements and so on.

As everyone helps to mentally direct their energy, lead the call to your group's guardians and/or primary deities. Ask them to be present for the ritual, explain that you are creating this group in their honor, and thank them for coming.

Next, state your group's purpose for existing. This can be previously written out, or each member can proclaim what they believe the group's function to be. End with "So Mote It Be" or whatever "Amen" sort of affirmation your group uses.

Purify the ritual area with incense and salt water—any members who wish to can do this step. Remember to cense and asperge each other as well.

Have everyone present bless the items you will be burying and/or hanging on the walls. This can be done all at once, or pass the items to each person in turn so they can add their energy.

Now select four people, one for each direction (if you have enough people, or else double up tasks), and have them bury the items that are sacred or special to the group at the four corners of the ritual space (this can also be done in a potted plant). Alternatively, or in addition to this, hang items or images on the four walls of the space that depict the four elements as your tradition or group dictates.

When everything is in place, raise energy with the group to create sacred space both on the astral and physical planes. You can use music, clapping and chanting, dance, or whatever your group works with best to raise energy. At the peak moment, have everyone hold the energy and visualize the temple space as glowing with light. Ring a bell or chime (an "energy chime" works very well for this) and have people continue to hold this image while channeling energy to the creation of the temple space. Let the sound die away completely until there is only silence, then say, "It is done. Our temple has been created."

Have everyone hold hands, hum a single note together for about a minute, then ground the energy to connect the people to the temple and the temple to the Earth.

Give the space a libation and blessing with the cakes and ale, then enjoy your food and drink, giving everyone a chance to chat pleasantly, but don't let it go on too long or it will become unfocused and the energy will dissipate. Close the circle and dismiss your guardians or deities as you usually do this. Say, "Merry meet, merry part, and merry meet again" or whatever ending is traditional for your group to indicate that the ritual is over.

VII

BLESSINGS
AND
HONORINGS

New Car and Safe Travel

WHERE: In the garage or outside

CAST: HP/S (also four directional priest/esses, optional)

MINIMUM NUMBER OF PARTICIPANTS: One

RITUAL DRESS: Your choice

PROPS: Drawstring pouch, mint and comfrey leaves, quartz point, carnelian stone, aquamarine stone, malachite stone, paper and pen, protection oil (purchased or formulate your own)

ALTAR SETUP: One small altar with the necessities off to one side, four small directional altars with the appropriate colored candle (yellow, red, blue, or green) and gemstone (East = quartz point, South = carnelian, West = aquamarine, North = malachite)

NOTES: This ritual should be performed as soon as possible after the acquisition of the new vehicle. Just before the ritual is to begin, the owner must wash and clean the car thoroughly inside and out.

Perform basic housekeeping such as announcements and so on.

Have everyone encircle the car and cast the circle as you usually would with the car in the middle. Cense and asperge the car inside and out, then cense and asperge all the charm ingredients (pouch, leaves, stones, and so on). Place the mint and comfrey leaves at the bottom of the pouch.

Now call to the elements (or, if using elemental priest/esses, have them call to their assigned element). Beginning in the East, light the yellow candle and say:

"Spirits of the East, you of new beginnings and of travel, bless and protect this car and those who ride inside it. Open the way ahead for them, remove obstacles, and help them to always get where they're going. So mote it be."

Place the quartz point inside the pouch and move on to South, lighting the red candle and saying:

"Spirits of the South, you of energy and protection, bless and protect this car and those who ride inside it. Keep them safe from harm and help them avoid damage and trouble. So mote it be."

Place the carnelian stone inside the pouch and move on to West, lighting the blue candle and saying:

"Spirits of the West, you of peace and ease of movement, bless and protect this car and those who ride inside it. Help them get where they need to go easily and help this vehicle to operate smoothly always. So mote it be."

Place the aquamarine stone inside the pouch and move on to North, lighting the green candle and saying:

"Spirits of the North, you of the crossroads and paths both light and dark, bless and protect this car and those who ride inside it. Help the driver to remain grounded at all times and help other drivers to act in a safe and grounded manner. May they always find their way safely. So mote it be."

Place the malachite stone inside the pouch and close it up. Say the charm "No breakdowns, no tickets, no trouble of any kind" out loud as you hold the pouch over the car. Write the same words on the paper, then place the paper into the pouch and say the charm again as you place the pouch inside the car. Good locations for the pouch are inside the glove compartment or under the driver's seat. If it's legal to do so in your area, you can also hang the pouch from the rearview mirror if it's small enough and does not interfere with the driver's view. The car owner should also say these words before getting in the car each time if possible.

Anoint the car with protection oil where you feel it necessary to do so, such as on the front fender, the roof, the driver's door, and the rear bumper. Now have everyone in your group hold hands and encircle the car. Everyone should direct protection energy at the car for about a minute, then count to three and have everyone clap together once on "three" to seal the spell.

Thank the elements for their help in your own way, and open the circle in the same way that you cast it. Say, "Merry meet, merry part, and merry meet again" or whatever ending is traditional for your group to indicate that the ritual is over.

Peace

WHERE: Anywhere without distractions

CAST: HP/S

MINIMUM NUMBER OF PARTICIPANTS: One

RITUAL DRESS: HP/S wears white or another color that represents peace

SUGGESTED SONGS: "Peace on Earth" (unknown, found in the book *Circle of Song*) or "Om Shanti" (Hindu traditional) or "Peace I Ask of Thee, O River" by Glendora Gosling and Viola Wood, "By the Earth" by Elaine Silver

PROPS: Energy chime, butterflies for release (optional, outside only) or small bottles of bubble soap

ALTAR SETUP: One central altar with nothing on it but a single white flower in a bud vase and the necessities. A simple one-color altar cloth in a cool or neutral color may be used as well.

CAKES AND ALE: Cold spring water and shortbread squares

NOTES: None

Perform basic housekeeping such as announcements and so on. Ring the energy chime and allow the sound to dissipate completely. Cast the circle as you normally would, then call the four elements/watchtowers as you usually do this.

The HP/S gives a grounding focus meditation for the group, spoken slowly with a soothing voice:

"Be seated and be comfortable. Close your eyes and take a deep breath . . . and another . . . now take another and see that you are standing in front of a cave's entrance. It is dark inside the cave, but you are not afraid because it's just the kind of cave you like best, and you know that you are always safe here.

"You begin to walk down into the cool darkness, running your hands along the walls as you walk, feeling a slight breeze on your face and body. Somewhere ahead of you, you can make out a dim light.

"Several candles have been lit here, and you can see that it is a place where others have come to seek peace and leave prayers and blessings. On the walls are beautiful white quartz crystals that sparkle faintly in the dim light, and the air has a lovely fragrance that makes you happy.

You find a comfortable seat, sit down, and you close your eyes.

"In the darkness you can feel the cool breeze, velvety on your skin like a lover. You soak up the silence and peace of this place, and know that any time you need to find a bit of quiet, you can always come here to this cave of peace deep inside Mother Earth. *(pause)*

"Breathe deeply the fragrant air of the cavern, allowing it to penetrate all the way out to your fingers and toes. Feel them tingle with the love and peace and energy of the Earth. You begin to hear others make their way into the cavern, and you know that they are here for the same reason you are here. You are all kin in this peaceful place, and you welcome them.

"Now it is time to work magic with your kin, so when you are ready, open your eyes and be here now."

Ring the chime again, letting the sound fade away completely. Continue the ritual by saying:

"Today we will cast a spell of peace. We will concentrate on the quiet energies and strengths of the elements, calling on the infinite love and peace of the Great Spirit as well to help us send this energy out to the world. Let us hold hands and join in the circle, the unity of all humankind. . . .

"To the East we ask for the gentle dawn of understanding for that is the place of begin-nings . . . *(pause)* . . . to the South we ask for the quiet strength to carry on . . . *(pause)* . . . to the West we ask for love and empathy for all . . . *(pause)* . . . to the North we ask for the silence of the listening stones that we may hear what others need to tell us. *(pause)*

"Now let us sing the music of the spheres . . . the universal chord from which all life began, that we may spread this perfect balance over the Earth, that it may bring peace to all humankind."

All intone a single note, raising energy, letting it flow and ebb until it finally peaks and is released by all. Silently release the butterflies or blow the bubbles, watching them as they drift away. This signifies your energy and prayers for peace traveling to all parts of the Earth and beyond.

Now enjoy your shortbread and cold water, either remaining silent and prayerful or allowing some sharing and talking as you eat. When everyone has finished, lead them in the chant "Peace on Earth" or "Om Shanti," or in the song "Peace I Ask of Thee, O River."

Lead them back out of the cave with a brief meditation:

"Now everyone close your eyes once again . . . you are still in the wonderful crystal cave with your kinfolk . . . look around in this place at the beautiful faces looking back at you . . . know that you can always come back here when you need a peaceful place to go, a safe and quiet place to meditate or work magic.

"Say farewell to your kin . . . *(pause)* And now it's time to find your way back out. You see the tunnel that you came through before, and you enter its cool darkness, like a refreshing drink of water. . . . You run your hands along the walls, finding your way back out, and you begin to see a dim white light somewhere before you. Every step brings you closer to the entrance, and you begin to feel a familiar breeze caress your face.

You blink in the brightening light, closing your eyes which are used to the cave's candles and the dark tunnel. When you are ready, open your eyes and return to where you started, here in this physical place, and be here now."

Thank the elements and open the circle, then lead everyone in "By the Earth." Say, "Merry meet, merry part, and merry meet again" or whatever ending is traditional for your group to indicate that the ritual is over. 🌿

Pregnancy Blessing

WHERE: Your choice

CAST: HP/S, pregnant woman, father of the child, drummers (optional)

MINIMUM NUMBER OF PARTICIPANTS: Two if the father is not included

RITUAL DRESS: Your choice

SUGGESTED SONGS: "Earth My Body" (unknown), "We Are a Circle Within a Circle" by Rick Hamouris, "I Am Feeling Very Open" by Loren Graham, "Opening Up" (unknown)

PROPS: Besom; anointing oil such as lavender;

gift for the mother to be held during labor, such as a stuffed animal, medicine bag, or necklace

ALTAR SETUP: One main altar with the necessities plus taper or pillar candles for the Mother Goddess, Father God and a tealight for the baby's spirit

CAKES AND ALE: Your choice, pomegranates, foods that the mother prefers (don't use foods that she may be made ill by—the stomach acts strangely when pregnant).

Notes: This ritual, which may or may not include the father depending on the circumstances, may be performed at any point during the pregnancy. Have everyone bring a gift for the parent(s) and/or baby.

Perform basic housekeeping such as announcements and so on.

Sweep the ritual area with the besom to remove any possible harmful influences. Cast the circle by singing "Earth My Body" as you walk around once, then get everyone singing the chant, letting it go on as long as people like. Drumming for this is good too, so if you want to and you have drummers, make this a fun, celebratory session.

When the song is finished, call to mother and birthing deities, lighting the two larger candles on the altar as you do:

"Great Mother, Goddess of fertility, Bes the laughing dwarf who protects families, Artemis the comforter and midwife, Asherah [ash-er-ah] who gives birth, Tauret [tower-et] the protector of pregnant women, Ix Chel [eesh-chell] who rides the night sky as the moon, Parvati the mother of Ganesha . . . you with a thousand names and more . . . Mother Earth, Father Sky, we ask that you watch over [name of mother] and her family as their lives change forever."

Turn to the parent(s) and say:

"We honor the Mother Goddess in you. (We honor the Father God in you.) You are a part of the never-ending cycle of life and death and rebirth. You are another link in the chain between our ancestors and those yet to come. We honor you and your child today. Blessed Be."

Anoint the parents and lead everyone in "We Are a Circle Within a Circle." When the chant is done, ask the parents to be seated and comfortable if they aren't already sitting. Lead them on a short guided meditation to meet the spirit of their unborn child:

"Close your eyes, relax, and take a deep breath . . . be at peace. . . . Take another deep breath and picture yourself on a path. The path is the kind you like best, and you begin to walk . . . soon you see another path to your side, and see that the other parent of your child is walking there . . . soon the paths converge, and you are both walking together on this beautiful path.

"A little way up the path you see a light, rather like a will-o'-the-wisp that floats just above the ground. You walk up to the light, and the light comes to you . . . you see two bright eyes in the light, and then the face of a small child . . . yes, this is your child . . . what does the child say to you? (Pause for at least a minute.) What do you say to the child?" (Pause another minute.)

"This meeting isn't long, and you can come back here when you wish to talk with this spirit. Say goodbye for now, but know that you will be together again very soon. Turn and walk back up the path . . . back up the way you came . . . back to where the paths separate . . . back to your own paths . . . back to your own bodies. . . .

"Take a deep breath and feel your body now, feel this room, and be here now."

Have the parent(s) light the tealight on the altar that represents the child's spirit now. If they would like to, the parents may share what they experienced. Next, move into teaching some birthing chants, such as "I Am Feeling Very Open" and "Opening Up." The father, if involved, should learn these chants as well so that he can coach her and sing with her at the birth.

Serve the cakes and ale, then give the mother the gift that she will hold during labor and tell her its significance. This is the perfect time for everyone to present the parent(s) with their gifts as well.

When cakes and ale are done, get the group's attention and ask the room "What promises do you now make to this family and this child? Who will help to care for them after the birth? I promise to . . ." Get things started and give your promise to the parent(s), such as "I promise to provide spiritual guidance when you need me and to feed the cats for the first week." Let everyone speak and conclude by holding hands and singing "We Are a Circle Within a Circle" again (or a different chant if you prefer a little more variety).

Thank the Mother Goddess and Father God, thank the elements, and open up the circle. Say, "Merry meet, merry part, and merry meet again" or whatever ending is traditional for your group to indicate that the ritual is over.

Long-Distance Healing

WHERE: Outside or inside

CAST: HP/S

MINIMUM NUMBER OF PARTICIPANTS: One

RITUAL DRESS: Your choice

SUGGESTED SONGS: "May You Walk This Land" by
Elat Ophidia Alekner or "Let the Spirit Come
to You" by Anodea Judith

PROPS: Pitcher and large bowl, rose water, soft
hand towel

ALTAR SETUP: One main altar, off to the side, with
the necessities

CAKES AND ALE: Your choice—something earthy
and nourishing is best

NOTES: In the pitcher, use one part culinary rose
water (available at Middle Eastern markets or
very well-stocked grocery stores) and four parts
spring or distilled water

Perform basic housekeeping such as announcements and so on. Cense and asperge all participants. Cast the circle and call the elements in
whatever manner makes everyone feel the most
comfortable. Have each person in turn call to a
deity that they feel connected to and strengthened
by to join the circle of healing spirits.

State (or restate) why everyone has come
together—to heal [name of person] who is [name
of specific location]. Lead everyone in the song
"May You Walk This Land" or "Let the Spirit Come
to You." Gently direct the energy to the person in
question and let it flow and ebb as it wants.

Have everyone hold hands and hum a single
note together. After a few seconds, intone the person's name and weave it in with the single note,
letting this flow and ebb as it wants. When the last
of the sounds ebb away, gently let go of your
neighbor's hands.

Give the meditation healing with a brief
explanation:

"We will now be individually focusing on
[name] and healing her [or him] on the astral.
Close your eyes and relax, and take a deep
breath, blowing out all your concerns, personal
stuff, and other things that might hamper your

ability to heal. Take another breath and fill yourself with light from your deity's grace . . . breathe out any last bits of yourself and your own worries. Fill yourself with light, and prepare to be a healer.

"Let your physical body move as it wants to heal [name], moving your arms, hands, and even standing up if you feel the need. Use your second sight to see the illness on the astral plane, and use your divine light to help [name] be rid of it. The tools you need will be there in your hand when you need them as well, whether you need a broom to sweep the illness away, a basin of water to wash it away, a holy flame to burn it away . . . whatever you need, it will be provided for you.

"I will be silent now as you work to heal [name]."

Sit quietly for as much time as you sense the group needs to heal the person. When you sense any fatigue or otherwise feel the group is ready to move on, very quietly say:

"Our time is drawing to a close. Give [name] a final blessing, and finish your work. When you are ready, take a deep breath, return, and open your eyes."

When everyone has returned, describe the purpose of the pitcher:

"Now that we have healed [name], we must purify ourselves so that no disease lingers with us or finds it way back to her [or him]. This pitcher contains pure spring [or distilled] water and rose water to wash both our bodies and spirits clean from any illness."

Give the pitcher to the person on your right, going widdershins to banish the illness, and take up the basin, holding it under his or her hands so that he or she may pour the water over them and wash them. Alternatively, you may place the basin on the floor at his or her feet and help to pour the water over his or her hands. Give him or her the towel to dry his or her hands and move on to the next person. When everyone has washed their hands (including yourself!), move on to the cakes and ale, letting everyone use this time to ground themselves with food and perhaps discuss the working they just did.

When everyone is ready, have each person thank and dismiss his or her deity, then thank and dismiss the elements, then open the circle. Say, "Merry meet, merry part, and merry meet again" or whatever ending is traditional for your group to indicate that the ritual is over.

Thanking the Land Spirits

WHERE: Outside

CAST: HP/S and helper

MINIMUM NUMBER OF PARTICIPANTS: Two

RITUAL DRESS: Your choice

SUGGESTED SONGS: "Calling in the Spirits" (Native American), "Old Ones Hear Us" by Mujiba Cabugos or "All Beings" by Rashani, "By the Earth" (both verses) by Elaine Silver

PROPS: Rose water in a pitcher (dilute one part culinary rose water into five parts spring water), incense (sticks or over charcoal in a brazier you can carry), bullroarer (easily made with a slat of wood and some string as shown in the illustration), lyrics for songs if needed

ALTAR SETUP: Table in the East containing the ritual tools

CAKES AND ALE: Your choice

Perform basic housekeeping such as announcements and so on.

You and your helper go around the circle sunwise/clockwise/deosil, outside the ring of people, and purify/bless the area with the rose water and incense. Return the incense and rose water to the altar and pick up the bullroarer, saying:

"Please be seated. This is a bullroarer, a very old item that is found all over the world, including Africa, Australia, and America. It was used in some cultures to call people over long distances to a gathering, and some cultures used it to call in the spirits. We are here today to celebrate and honor the spirits of the land, so let's tell them that we would like them to come and be with us now by using the bullroarer and singing this song from the Cree tribe traditionally used for calling in the spirits of the four directions."

Start the "Calling in the Spirits" song and swing the bullroarer in time to the song. Swing it quickly over your head so that it makes its distinctive loud humming sound. Go through "Calling in the Spirits" four times, then stop both the song and the bullroarer.

Take the incense and blow it out into the air to the four directions. Now give a prayer of thanksgiving and blessing to the spirits:

Bullroarer construction

Bullroarer use

"Old Ones, ancient spirits of this place, creatures of the land, powers of the earth's magic, we have called out to you so that we may thank you. We thank you for letting us use your places, may we always keep them clean and beautiful. We thank you for your gifts to us, may we always give back to you in return. We thank you for sharing your secrets, may we always use this knowledge wisely. Old Ones, hear us now . . . we honor you and we thank you. We are all thankful for your gifts to us. I am thankful for _____ (say what you are thankful for)."

Turn to the person in the east and ask "what do you thank the Old Ones for?" Indicate that they are to respond out loud and prompt everyone in turn to speak out what they thank the spirits of the land for. When everyone has had a turn, say:

"You see how we love you and thank you, spirits of this place. We may not always say it aloud, we may not always show you, but we are people of the earth and we appreciate your gifts to us every day of our lives."

Turn to the group and start the chant "All Beings" or "Old Ones Hear Us". Drums are nice for this, but not essential. When the chant finally dies away or otherwise ends, give out the cakes and ale. When everyone has received theirs, give out a libation onto the ground and say:

"Old Ones, we give you this libation, this offering, so that you may be ever nourished . . . we give back to you what we receive. You bless us, so we bless you. Blessed be."

After the cakes and ale, give everyone a little bell and say:

"This bell is for you to communicate with the spirits of your land. Ring it to let the spirits know they are loved, or to call out to them, or hang it from a pretty ribbon so that the spirits can use it when they are near and wish to communicate with you."

Lead everyone in both verses of "By the Earth." Say, "Merry meet, merry part, and merry meet again" or whatever ending is traditional for your group to indicate that the ritual is over.

Hospital Healing

WHERE: Indoors

CAST: HP/S, priest/ess for each direction (optional)

MINIMUM NUMBER OF PARTICIPANTS: One

RITUAL DRESS: Your choice

PROPS: Compass, small bowl of salt water (real ocean water is nice), sprig of cedar, feather, crystal point, small bowl of fresh water, small dish of salt

CAKES AND ALE: Spring water

NOTES: In advance, let the hospital and staff know that you are the designated clergyperson for the patient in question, that you have his or her permission to minister to them (ideally you should obtain written permission in advance if the person is unable to vouch for you due to his or her condition, or you can try to obtain some kind of documentation or verification from family members or circlemates), and that you will be doing a healing ritual for them. Take the size of the space and privacy into account as well—if the room is large and it's not shared, you can bring the whole coven . . . if the room is tiny and has other patients present, you'll probably fly solo by necessity.

Before beginning any work, find out what the patient needs and how he or she feels about the ritual. Make any changes necessary and schedule the time that you will be conducting the ritual.

When you arrive, determine the cardinal directions and make a mental note of where East is (always use a compass in a hospital—they tend to be psychically disorienting, so even if you think you know, check anyway).

Take a moment to relax, then help everyone ground and center. Prepare the small bowl of salt water and, using the cedar sprig, gently asperge the patient, softly sprinkling or brushing the water over his or her body. Alternately, you may use a different healing herb or a feather to distribute the water.

Prepare the dishes of water and salt and set them aside at the ready. If you have the help of others, have them stand in the cardinal directions, otherwise make sure there's a place to put your objects where they won't be disturbed until the ritual is over.

Give the feather to the helper in the East, and say:

"Healing spirits of the East, soft breezes of change and newness, heal [name of patient] by sweeping away all disease, all illness, all pain. So mote it be."

Give the crystal point to the South helper and say:

"Healing spirits of the South, fires of strength and will, heal [name of patient] by burning away all disease, all illness, all pain. So mote it be."

Give the small bowl of water to the West helper and say:

"Healing spirits of the West, waters of healing and love, heal [name of patient] by washing away all disease, all illness, all pain. So mote it be."

Give the small dish of salt to the North helper and say:

"Healing spirits of the North, caves of rebirth and safety, heal [name of patient] by taking away all disease, all illness, all pain. So mote it be."

Now call to the Lord and Lady for healing:

"Loving and nurturing Mother, kind and protective Father, Lady and Lord, your children call to you. [Name of patient] calls to you. Let your healing powers enter us . . . let your love and light enter us . . . let us burn away the illness . . . let us transform damaged flesh into healthy flesh . . . help us make [patient] whole again."

Have everyone around the bed hold hands or, if it's just you and the patient, hold his or her hands or place your hands above (not touching) the afflicted area. Say: "Now let us gather and direct these gifts to help heal [patient]." Begin to hum a single note very softly and close your eyes, using the energies of the elements and Lady and Lord to heal and transform the illness. Continue doing this until the moment seems right to stop—you'll know when.

The patient will likely feel a tingling or buzzing around the body, as if floating on a cloud. Now say: "From sky to root, bring the energy down into the earth to seal the spell." Very, very gently touch the patient and blow on him or her very softly from his head down to his feet. Ground the energy securely, and ask the patient how he or she feels. If the patient still feels really "floaty," you may need to do a firmer grounding or other work—discern the needs and act accordingly. He or she may also need to eliminate, which is a good sign. If this is the case, allow a few minutes of silent privacy, then return when he or she is ready to partake of the water.

Close the ritual simply:

"Great powers of the elements, loving Lord and Lady, we ask that you continue to heal and watch over [patient] as [he or she] needs your help. Your child serves you well through faith, love, trust, and beauty. May your gifts be with [him or her] always. So mote it be."

Cats and the People Who Love Them

WHERE: Inside

CAST: HP/S

MINIMUM NUMBER OF PARTICIPANTS: One

RITUAL DRESS: Your choice

SUGGESTED SONGS: Variation on "Snake Woman" by Reclaiming

PROPS: Statues and images of Bast for the altar

ALTAR SETUP: One very large table opposite the entrance to the ritual area. The altar should use green and brown altarcloths and feature images of Bast, some live catnip plants if possible or flowers, incense, and a green or white candle. A few natural brown rabbit furs would look nice on the altar as well, and give it a tactile, furry dimension.

CAKES AND ALE: Cornbread (made in a cat-shaped pan if possible) and milk/soy milk

NOTES: Make sure everyone brings pictures of their cats, living and/or dead, and offerings to both their spirits and to Bast, such as favorite toys, catnip mice, and so on. You can also have a basket of extra goodies on hand for people who didn't bring anything so they can participate.

Perform basic housekeeping such as announcements and so on. Begin the ritual by saying:

"Hello everyone, and welcome. Today we're honoring one of the most popular animals for a Witch to have around the house—the cat. Cats have been with us for thousands of years, and will be with us for many thousands more. Sometimes that special cat comes along that helps us in our magical workings, the familiar who can see into our souls. If you've had very many cats in your life, some of them have probably passed on . . . and you probably have at least one now. We'll recognize all the cats, past and present, who have graced our lives with their special ways.

"Let's all come up to the altar and place our kitty items on it. Have a good time, be creative, and if you didn't bring anything, come up anyway to visit and enjoy the altar."

Allow some time for people to visit the altar. When everyone is finished, continue by saying:

"As I've said, cats have been with us for thousands of years. They come to us from ancient

Egypt, descendants of the wild desert cats who were tamed and brought into the temples, especially the temple of Bast, the Lady of the Nile delta. Bast is usually shown as a cat-headed woman or in full catform, and she is often shown with kittens, for her role as goddess of the family, a sistrum, indicating her love of music and dance, and bedecked with jewelry including gold ear and nose rings. Bast is also a tremendous healing goddess of transformation and duality, which is why she is often shown with a scarab, the Egyptian symbol of transformation.

"And speaking of transformation . . . in the European Middle Ages, the cat was changed into an agent of the devil along with the Witches. It was no longer safe for a Pagan to have a cat, as they were often killed on sight during the Burning Times, so many turned to owning hard-to-see black cats instead, leading to our current stereotype of the gnarled, green-skinned crone with a black cat.

"This wholesale slaughter of cats backfired, however . . . without cats to keep them in control, the population of mice, rats, and other vermin not only caused food storage and disease problems, the fleas that live on mice and rats carried the bubonic plague rapidly across Europe.

"In more recent times, the cat has not only become accepted again, but a much-loved part of our society and our lives. Organizations have been formed solely for their protection and safety (which I hope you will donate generously to if you can), and millions, if not billions of dollars are spent annually on feline vet bills all over the world.

"As I'm sure you already know, cats are natural healers, both physically and spiritually. Many studies have shown that stroking a cat lowers blood pressure, and cat owners are generally healthier, live longer, and are more relaxed people. Cats are our familiars, companions, friends, totems, and alter egos. I can't imagine being a Witch in a world without cats!

"Let's speak the names of our cats, past and present, to honor their spirits and their gifts to us. I'll start with my own . . ."

Name your cat(s) and indicate that others are to do the same. When it appears that everyone has finished naming their cat(s), continue the ritual with the "Snake Woman" song variation:

"Now we're going to have some fun with a popular chant—'Snake Woman' by the Reclaiming Collective. You probably know it . . . (*Sing the tune: "Snake Woman shedding her skin . . . shedding, shedding, shedding her skin . . . Snake Woman shedding her skin . . . shedding, shedding, shedding her skin."*) So what we're going to do, and I expect you good people to help out with this by shouting out your verse idea when we come back around, is make it Cat Woman. I'll start."

Begin with "Cat Woman shedding her fur . . ." and sing through two times with everyone as above. Some ideas, if people don't come up with their own or run out of ideas, are: sharpening claws, coughing up hair, purring real loud, feeling so soft, meowing for food, catching the birds, licking herself, curling up snug, etc.

Next, it's time for cakes and ale. Ask one or two participants to help give out the cornbread and milk. Allow several minutes for people to enjoy the refreshments and chat a bit. As this portion draws to a close, place some of the food and drink on the altar and say:

"Great Lady Bast, you who embrace the mysterious nature of the cat, and you who watch over your kittens, please accept our offering.

May we continue to learn from your children and be comforted by the cats in our lives."

Turning back to the group, say:

"Let us give thanks to the spirit of the cat in all its forms. Take a moment of silence now to meditate on how cats have blessed your life."

Allow a minute or two for people to meditate on this, then say:

"Cats are special and unique creatures in so many ways, and they bless us as we love them. May it ever be so. Now it's time to get back and stroke their fur once again. Before you leave, don't forget to reclaim your items from the altar and acknowledge Bast."

Finish by saying, "Merry meet, merry part, and merry meet again" or whatever ending is traditional for your group to indicate that the ritual is over. ❧

New Baby Blessing

Where: Outside or Inside, depending on the
weather

Cast: HP/S, parent(s) of child, child

Minimum Number of Participants: Three

Ritual Dress: Your choice

Suggested Songs: "Ib Ache" (African traditional,
also called "Eeb Ashay"), "You Are Beautiful,"
"We Sing with Mother Earth," or "I Am an
Acorn" by Carol Johnson

Props: A very gentle, nonallergenic anointing oil
(such as plain olive oil, rose oil cut with
almond oil, and so on . . . diluted rose water
may also be used), a small dish of sugar (*not*
honey, which can be deadly for infants)

Altar Setup: One main altar with the necessities

Cakes and Ale: Fortune cookies and milk (also
provide soy milk if needed)

Notes: Have everyone bring a small gift for the
baby, preferably something to see the infant
through life and help him or her to learn
about the world, such as nature picture books,
charms to hang in the nursery, rattles that can
double later on as ritual shakers, and so on.

Provide a pretty pouch for everyone to place
their fortune cookie fortunes in to be given to
the child.

Perform basic housekeeping such as announcements and so on.

Cast the circle and call the elements as you usually do this, but leave the parent(s) and baby outside the ritual area. If they are in another room,
call them to the edge of the circle.

Asperge and/or cense everyone in the circle,
starting to the left of the "doorway" where they
will be admitted. When you come back around to
the door again, face the parent(s) and ask: "Who is
this newcomer to our community? Why have you
brought him [or her] here?" Assuming the answer
is to your satisfaction, asperge and/or cense them
and admit them into the circle.

State to the group the purpose of the working:

"We have a newcomer, both to our community and to the world. We are all here today to
witness this and to welcome her [or him], to

bless her, to thank her for gifting us with her spirit, trusting us to care for her, and choosing to be here now.

"This new child is a precious gift, and is here to learn much as well as teach much. We honor her parents for the work they have already done for her, and for the work they will be doing for her. It is not easy to be a parent . . . it's perhaps the most difficult job in the universe, and so we honor you. *(Anoint the heart(s) of the parent(s).)*

"Let us now present this child to the powers of the world, that they may know each other better."

Have the parent hold the baby out to the East and say:

"Spirits of the East, Powers of the East, Beings of the East, we present this child to you. Bless him [or her] and teach him your secrets that he may walk in beauty always. So mote it be."

Repeat this for the other directions, then have the parent lay the baby on the ground. Kneel beside the child with one hand on the ground and say:

"Earth Mother, we present this child to you. Bless her [or him] and teach her your secrets that she may walk in beauty always. So mote it be."

Have the parent hold the child aloft toward the sky and repeat for Sky Father/the Sun, raising your hand to the sky as you do so. Have the parent hold the child close in the center, and say:

"We hold this child in the center of all that he [or she] may understand that balance is the key to all. Finding the center in himself, he becomes a balanced person. Finding the center among others, he becomes a fair and just person. Finding the center in the world, he becomes a spiritual person. May he always walk in beauty and balance, all the days of his life. So mote it be."

Using the anointing oil or diluted rose water, anoint the baby gently on the crown of his or her head and say:

"Blessed be your mind, that you may attain the knowledge you need in this lifetime to grow.

(Anoint the forehead and say:) "Blessed be the magic within and without you, may you recognize your gifts and use them wisely.

(Anoint the throat and say:) "Blessed be your voice, that it may speak words of wisdom, words of power, words of magic, and words of blessing to others.

(Anoint the heart and say:) "Blessed be your heart, may you always love and be loved in beauty.

(Anoint the genitals and say:) "Blessed be your sex, the gift to create new life and give pleasure to others. May you use it wisely.

(Anoint the feet and say:) "Blessed be your feet, that you may walk a path that is filled with beauty, with love, with balance, and with magic. So mote it be."

If the child is to receive a craft name, ask the parents to name him or her so now in front of the group, otherwise use the child's legal name. Take a small pinch of sugar and place it in the baby's mouth, saying:

"Taste the sweetness of life, [name]! The world is full of delights and your future is filled with endless possibilities. Rejoice and be welcomed!"

Lead everyone in the song "Ib Ache," "You Are Beautiful," "We Sing with Mother Earth," "I Am an Acorn" (changing it to "You Are . . ."), or another appropriate song to honor the child. Next, have each person give their gift to the child, and then move on to the cookies and milk. As each person opens a fortune cookie, he or she stands and reads it out loud, then presents it to the child. When everyone's done, put the fortunes into the pouch and give to the baby as a group gift.

Thank the elements and open the circle in your usual manner. Say, "Merry meet, merry part, and merry meet again" or whatever ending is traditional for your group to indicate that the ritual is over.

VIII

PERSONAL TRANSFORMATION

Four Rounds Inside the Sweat Lodge

WHERE: Outside

CAST: HP/S, fire tender

MINIMUM NUMBER OF PARTICIPANTS: Two

RITUAL DRESS: Your choice, but you'll probably want a swimsuit or light cotton breathable clothing to stay as cool as possible, or your group could go skyclad

SUGGESTED SONGS: "It's the Blood of the Ancients" by Charlie Murphy, "Old Ones" by Earl Edward Bates, "We Are a Circle" by Rick Hamouris, "In the Fire" by Cynthia R. Crossen, "We Are An Old People" by Morning Feather, "'Tis a Gift to Be Simple" (traditional Shaker), "Let the Spirit Come to You" by Anodea Judith, "We Are the Flow" by Shekhinah Mountainwater, "Carry It Home" by Betsy Rose, "O Great Spirit" by Adele Getty

PROPS: You'll need to construct a sweat lodge and have a fire-safe place to use it outdoors. See Chapter 4 of my previous book *The Veil's Edge* for complete instructions on the construction and use of a traditional sweat lodge (brief instructions appear below). You'll also need enough wood for a very hot fire to last about two hours, sixteen fist-sized rocks (be *sure* they can be heated to red- or orange-hot and then cooled suddenly without shattering—test them first), a shovel, a bucket of water and dipper, sprigs of artemisia sage or California mugwort sage to give out (do not substitute—these are cooling herbs for people to use if they start getting overheated), and towels for people to sit on. If anyone in your group wears glasses or wishes to remove jewelry before entering, a towel-lined basket is nice to have on hand to hold these things.

CAKES AND ALE: Your choice, preferably using nonalcoholic beverages, since alcohol can affect the body's ability to cool itself, which is vitally important for a sweat session. Make this a potluck feast for afterward—people will need to ground themselves with food and drink after the sweat. Make cold water available to people upon exiting the lodge, however.

NOTES: Have people bring drums if they like for after the sweat. This ritual is intended for a smaller group since there is limited room inside a sweat lodge. Depending on the size of your lodge, about 6 to 12 people is probably optimal. It is based on the basic model of some traditional Native American sweats but is *not* an actual traditional ceremony, so if you wish to alter parts of this ritual to suit your group, feel free to do so. Be sure you read through the entire text below before running this ritual.

To build a sweat lodge, you will need a flat earthen area with a nearby space suitable (or construction of a firepit, about twenty sturdy yet flexible saplings such as willow or maple, rope, many blankets to cover it, and a shovel. Dig a large pit in the center of your lodge area for the hot stones. Bury the larger butt ends of the saplings in the earth and bend them over to form a dome about four to five feet high(see illustration). Tie the top and sides of the dome securely and cover it with blankets so that no light is visible (you may also use one tarp if you're short on blankets, but DO NOT bury the ends so that some air can still come into the lodge and DO NOT use sheet plastic). Use blankets for a flap door, securing them with clamps or clothespins if necessary.

In advance, assess the ability of all participants to handle the extreme conditions of a sweat lodge and adjust accordingly—if everyone is physically able, run a hot sweat; if some of your members are unable to tolerate the heat and lack of fresh air, use fewer

blankets on the lodge and make the rounds very short. Traditionally, people should stay for all four rounds, but if someone feels ill or otherwise needs to leave, you should certainly allow him or her to do so.

Also in advance, decide on a "five minute signal" with your fire tender, who remains outside the lodge at all times. It can be a single drum beat, or one rock hitting another rock, whatever you will hear inside the lodge during the sweat to let you know when ten minutes has passed during a round so that you can judge when to end it and open the flap.

Your fire tender must be able to skillfully

A simple traditional sweat lodge is relatively easy to construct with stout young willows, vines or rope to hold it together, and blankets to cover it completely.

handle a shovel containing red-hot rocks and keep the fire going safely at all times, so pick just the right person for this extremely important job. Start the fire at least a half hour before the start of ritual—an hour before is even better. Pile the rocks in the center of the fire pit (the one outside the lodge, not inside) and build a large, hot bonfire over them. They are not ready unless they're completely glowing red or even orange.

Perform basic housekeeping such as announcements and so on.

Introduce the ritual by giving a brief explanation of what will happen:

"As you enter, take a sprig of sage. If you feel too hot at any time during the sweat, you can breathe the cool fragrance and be refreshed. You can also reach behind you at the edge of the covering and find some cool air with your hands if you need to.

"As you enter, move to your left around the central pit and continue around to find your seat. If you can't handle much heat, sit closer to the door, which will be opened every fifteen minutes or so. At that point anyone who needs to may leave, but you will not be admitted back inside. Now, let's begin."

Usher everyone inside, then take the last seat to the left of the door and bring the bucket of water and dipper with you. Give a brief grounding for everyone before starting the sweat:

"Relax, become comfortable, and feel your connection to Mother Earth. Feel the dirt underneath your body . . . see the dome that covers us made from Earth's branches . . . smell the sage in your hand . . . soon the bones of the Earth will come inside and give us their wisdom. . . . Take a deep breath, and be ready to hear it. Be ready to give away and to receive. Take a deep breath and be ready."

The fire tender now uses the shovel to pick out four red-hot rocks and places them in the central pit, then the door flap is closed. Dip some water from the bucket and sprinkle it over the rocks to release steam. Begin the first round by honoring the spirits and ancestors:

"Feel yourself floating in the darkness. Feel the steam gathering on your body, your face. . . . Feel your kinship with those around you. . . . Feel your kinship with all life. Let us now go around the circle and honor the spirits, honor our ancestors, honor the life that we are brother and sister to. If you don't wish to say anything, simply say 'All My Relations,' which honors them. I'll begin . . ."

When everyone has commented or said "All My Relations," sing and chant until the round is over. Good songs for this section include "It's the Blood of the Ancients," "Old Ones," and "We Are a Circle." Call to the fire tender to open the flap and let people relax for about three to five minutes.

The fire tender brings in four more rocks and closes the flap. Sprinkle more water over the new hot rocks and begin the second round:

> "We all have 'stuff' . . . stuff that we don't need or that's maybe hurting us inside. Sometimes we hang on to this stuff because it feels comfortable and familiar . . . sometimes we want to get rid of this stuff but don't know how to do it. Well, let your body sweat it out right now. Sweat and tears are full of toxins . . . full of stuff that your body needs to get rid of . . . let your body and your soul sweat away the junk you don't need anymore. Sit in the darkness, in the silence, and let it leave you now."

Sprinkle some more water to generate more steam, and allow people to sit in silence for about ten minutes. At the five-minute warning sound from your fire tender, let people talk about what they got rid of if they wish to, or lead everyone in a chant. Good chants or songs for this section include "In the Fire," and "We Are an Old People." Call to the fire tender to open the flap and let people relax for about three to five minutes as needed.

The fire tender brings in four more rocks and closes the flap. Sprinkle more water over the new hot rocks and begin the third round:

"We have honored our ancestors and kin . . . we have given away what we need to be rid of . . . now we need to fill the void created by getting rid of stuff with our wishes and prayers for the future. Take some time now and fill yourself with all the good dreams of tomorrow . . . think about what you need most in your life, what will bring the most happiness . . . or think about the needs of others, perhaps healing or good fortune. *(pause—about two minutes)*

"Now speak those things out loud. We are all anonymous here in the darkness . . . we are all kin . . . speak your prayers and they will become reality, for the spoken word is one of the most powerful things in the universe. I'll start. . . ."

Speak your prayers, wishes, etc., and then go around the circle, letting everyone speak or say "All My Relations" if they have nothing to add. Good songs for this round include "'Tis a Gift to Be Simple," "Let the Spirit Come to You" and "We Are the Flow." Call to the fire tender to open the flap and let people relax for about three to five minutes as needed.

The fire tender brings in four more rocks and closes the flap. Sprinkle more water over the new hot rocks and begin the fourth and final round:

> "I know we are getting tired, but this is the place of visions now . . . fatigue, sensory deprivation, heat, sweat, lack of air . . . these things

take away our physical body and release our minds to seek visions. Let your mind wander now . . . see who or what comes to you . . . listen now to their message for you . . . *(pause— about ten minutes)*

"Say farewell if you are still conversing with someone or if you need to come back from a vision. . . . Breathe deeply into your sage . . . let the cool herb bring you back to yourself so that we can sing songs of thanksgiving and blessings."

Good songs for this round include "Carry It Home" and "O Great Spirit."

Now give a short closing prayer:

"Ancestors, Old Ones, Great Spirit . . . we thank you for sustaining us on this journey, for the sweat lodge is always a journey. We sing to you, we give thanks to you . . . may you always lend us your strength and help us find the path."

Call to the fire tender to open the flap and let people exit, reminding them to continue the circle around to their left until the door is reached. Let them cool off a bit, make sure everyone's okay and has water, then enjoy the potluck feast! You might also want to blow off some steam (pun intended) with a lively drumming circle if people would like to do this.

Tree of Life/Kabbalah

WHERE: Outside (indoors if necessary)
CAST: HP/S, four directional priest/esses
MINIMUM NUMBER OF PARTICIPANTS: Five
RITUAL DRESS: Your choice
SUGGESTED SONGS: "Standing Like a Tree" by Betsy Rose
PROPS: Basket or bowl, tree agate beads or tumbled stones

ALTAR SETUP: One main altar with the necessities
CAKES AND ALE: Your choice
NOTES: Ideally, this ritual should be performed with a living tree in the center of the ritual space. If you cannot do the ritual outdoors with a naturally growing tree, use a large potted living tree such as a ficus (in the same family as the Buddhist Bodhi tree). Place the bowl or

basket of tree agate at the base of the tree. If you prefer different wordings for the sacred space creation, alternative versions of the LBRP are available on many internet websites.

Perform basic housekeeping such as announcements and so on. Cense and asperge the working space and everyone present. Facing East, perform the Kabbalistic Cross. Intone "Ateh" [*ah-teh*] as you use your athame or fingers of your power hand to bring the Light of Spirit down into your crown. Intone "Malkuth" [*mal-kooth*] as you then bring the Light into your heart and then down below your feet into infinity. Intone "Ve-Geburah" [*vay geb-ooh-rah*] and extend your right arm, directing the Light through your right arm and out into infinity. Intone "Ve-Gedulah" [*vay ged-ooh-lah*] and extend your left arm, directing the Light through your left arm and out into infinity. Intone "Le Olamh" [*lay oh-lam*] as you bring the Light into your center, visualizing a golden glow there and intoning "Amen" to finish the ritual.

Now perform the Lesser Banishing Ritual of the Pentagram (LBRP, given below) at each of the four directions. The words are:

"YVHV! [*yah-ho-vah* or *yah-way*] Adonai! [*ah-doh-nai*] Eheieh! [*ee-heh-ee-eh*] Aglah! [*ah-glah*]"

At each direction draw the banishing pentagram of that element: East/Air begins at upper left and draws across to upper right, South/Fire starts at lower right and draws up to the top, West/Water

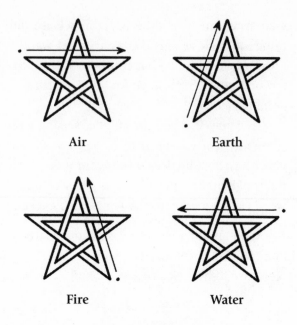

Air   **Earth**

Fire   **Water**

Banishing Pentagrams

starts at upper right and draws to the upper left, and North/Earth starts at the lower left and draws up to the top.

Cast the circle as you normally do this. Now have each priest/ess invoke the archangels of the four directions. The words are:

"Before me Raphael [*rah-fay-el*], behind me Gabriel [*gah-bree-el*], on my right hand Michael [*mik-ay-el*], on my left hand Auriel [*ah-ree-el*], about me flame the pentagrams, and above me shines the six-rayed star."

In turn as they recite the words, the East priest/ess draws the invoking pentagram of Air (begin at

Air   Earth

Fire   Water

Invoking Pentagrams

upper right and draw toward the upper left), the South priest/ess draws the invoking pentagram of Fire (begin at the top and draw down to lower right), the West draws the invoking pentagram of Water (begin at upper left and draw toward upper right), and the North draws the invoking pentagram of Earth (begin at the top and draw down toward lower left).

To call the elements, use the imagery of the four Archangels that were called upon in the LBRP:

"In the East we call to the Archangel Raphael. Guard us with your arrows, fan us with your wings. Ward us and protect us! So mote it be.

"In the South we call to the Archangel Michael. Defend us with your sword, set our wills ablaze with your fires of transformation. Ward us and protect us! So mote it be.

"In the West we call to the Archangel Gabriel. Awaken us with your horn, heal us with your compassion. Ward us and protect us! So mote it be.

"In the North we call to the Archangel Auriel. Protect us with your shield, help us grow in your garden. Ward us and protect us! So mote it be."

Give a brief history of the Tree of Life/World Tree/Kabbalah as seen in many cultures:

"Today we will explore and honor the Tree of Life, also called the World Tree in some traditions. We are focusing on a Kabbalistic approach for this ritual and meditation, but virtually every culture on earth has recognized and honored the idea of the Tree of Life in their spirituality.

"In Norse mythology it is called Yggdrasil and represents nine worlds or planes. It is the tree that Odin hung from to attain knowledge. From Germanic belief we have received the tradition of the Yule tree, the evergreen decorated with ornaments and lights to honor everlasting life and the sun's rebirth. To Buddhists, the Bodhi tree is significant as the place that Siddhartha achieved nirvana.

"To the Christians and Jews, the 'tree of life' is the other holy tree in the garden of Eden, the one that grants immortality. The Celts saw the 'tree of life' as the embodiment of the integrity of their people, with its roots stretching into the lower world and branches reaching into the upper world.

"The native peoples of Australia, Hawaii, Alaska, the Americas, all honor certain tree species as life-giving and as teachers, using them in sacred ways and to build their holy buildings. Science sees the branchings of plant and animal species as the 'tree of life.' Even in the *Lord of the Rings* by J.R.R. Tolkien we see lots of tree symbolism and elevation in which they are considered holy and magical things.

"The trees have much to teach us . . . but one holy tree in particular is the Tree of Life. It is symbolic, yes, but it is often through symbols that we can understand the nature of Spirit. The tree reaches down into the Underworld and up to heaven . . . trees live much longer than we do and can be virtually immortal, with some living for thousands of years—the oldest known tree is a California bristlecone pine recorded to be 4,767 years old, which is older than the pyramids in Egypt.

"It is this kind of eternal life force and ancient wisdom that help us understand the significance of trees, and especially the symbolism of the eternal World Tree or Tree of Life. Let us now go on a journey through the Tree of Life, beginning at its base, traveling up to the mys-teries of heaven. Close your eyes and become comfortable.

"Let us begin in the earth with Malkuth [*mal-kooth*]. This is the Earth Mother that gives us our life. As you stand before the Tree of Life, you stand on Malkuth. Your body is the flesh and blood of Malkuth. You see the material form of the Tree, its roots going into the ground . . . moss growing all around . . . grasses and plants growing all around . . . this is the gateway to both the tree's mysteries and to the Underworld. Today we look upward into its branches and see bright spheres glowing there . . . and we start on the journey upward.

"The next place we climb to is Yesod [*yeh-sod*], the Foundation of Life. This is the place of sex, of conception, and the beginning of the spiritual path. It is above the material world and connects it to the world of the spirit. You look through the branches of the tree above you and see the moon, shining her holy light upon you, and you feel your soul begin to stir. *(pause)*

"Climb upward again, this time to your left, and you shall find Hod, the place of intellect and logic. This is where the secret rites come from . . . this is where the poets find their muse . . . what does it have to teach you now? *(pause)*

"Climb across the tree to the other side, to the right, and you shall find Netzach, [*net-zak*] the place of emotion. Hod and Netzach can be considered opposites, but often they work together. Enlightenment is found in the center, not to one side or the other, so we must balance Hod with Netzach. Call forth your emotions now . . . what do you feel? *(pause)*

"Between Hod and Netzach, and higher still in the tree, is Tiphareth (tiff-er-eth), the place of beauty. The sun now shines upon your face and hair, and shows you the beauty of the world, laid out before you like a tapestry. What do you see? *(pause)*

"Climb again to your left to encounter Geburah [*geb-ur-ah*], the place of severity. You are the warrior who avenges evil. You are on the battlefield, fighting the enemies of enlightenment. You cut away the disease so that beauty may prevail. Your sword is razor sharp . . . what do you cut with it? *(pause)*

"Climb across now to Chesed [*chess-ed*], the balance of Geburah, which is mercy. This is the force that stays the sword . . . the laughing spirit of kindness that brings water to the injured. A smile brings beauty to the harshest face, and restores the balance. To whom or what do you show mercy now? *(pause)*

"You step forth to climb higher, but your foot slips and you fall. Instead of simply falling to the ground, you continue falling. 'When will this end?' you think to yourself as the darkness envelops you, and still you fall into the abyss. This is Daath [*dah-th*], the hidden place, the chasm of knowledge. Somewhere below you is

the material world, the balance of severity and mercy, intelligence and emotion . . . all these things fall away from you now. You see nothing . . . you feel nothing . . . you simply are. This is the shadow . . . this is naked knowledge of the divine, where you must walk if you seek enlightenment. This is the blackened scrying mirror. What do you see? *(pause)*

"A shining hand reaches for yours . . . a woman's hand . . . and you stop falling. You sit now in the lap of the Goddess who soothes your fears, for she understood that you needed Her. This is Binah [*bee-nah*], the Great Mother of all, matriarch of mankind . . . and you begin to understand the ways of love, creation, and purpose. Listen now to her words, which will help you to understand your purpose for being. *(pause—about a minute)*

"She lifts you up and you see that you are near the uppermost branches of the tree. Below you there is darkness, and above you there is light. But instead of lifting you up into the light, Binah gives you over to the Father, who is called Chockmah [*chok-mah*]. He is the place of wisdom, the other half of understanding. He is all-knowing . . . the third eye . . . that which directs creation's spark. Sit with Him now and see past, present, and future. *(pause—about a minute)*

"Chockmah lifts you up now. You are lifted toward the final light, the brightest light of heaven, the light at the very top of the tree of life. You realize that His hands no longer hold you, and that you simply exist in the light, floating weightless in Kether [keh-ther], the source, the all-being. This is the holy of holies, the great mystery. The light surrounds you, penetrates you, fills you up with holy being and perfection. You are one . . . you shine forth as the light shines forth. Simply experience this perfection. (pause—about a minute)

"You are still alive, and you still have a physical form that must be remembered. You cannot remain in Kether, but you can bring some of that light back with you. This is the perfection of creation . . . the potential that you need in your life. You feel Chokmah's hands upon you once again, and He helps you to direct this pure energy. . . . (pause)

"Now Binah takes you back and cradles you once again, helping you to understand what must be done. (pause)

"This triad of spirit, wisdom, and understanding have built a bridge for you. . . . You look into the darkness and over the abyss you see a sturdy bridge that enables you to pass over the chasm called Daath. Walk over this bridge now and know that if you fall, the triad will lift you up again and help you find your way. (pause)

"Happiness bubbles forth as you see that you have made it across and are beginning your journey back down the tree to its roots. Chesed will always be with you, showing mercy to you so that you may show mercy to others on your path.

"Balancing this softness is the strength and power of Geburah, who knows when to fight and when to sever. This power is that which sees the final goals of your workings and does what it takes to get you there.

"You climb back down the tree to Tiphareth, seeing even more fully than before the beauty of yourself, the beauty of the world, and the beauty of magic. This is your center, your heart. Take this balance with you as you climb down to Netzach.

"'Love conquers all' is the message of Netzach, where you achieve mastery over your emotions and become stronger, yet learn to love even more. Hod is next, the place of intellect and thought. The balance is complete, and you know what to do with the light that you were given.

"You climb down to Yesod and the light is given form . . . the spark of conception is transformed here . . . manifestation has begun. And so you lightly touch the ground and reunite with Malkuth, the physical realm. What you need to do is here now. . . . You need to come back to your physical body and finish the working that you have started. You are pregnant with it—now is the time to gestate your working and see it through until it is born. When you are ready, awaken back in your physical body and continue the ritual in Malkuth, where you will receive a gift to hold the power of your working."

When most people are back, let them know about the tree agate:

"At the base of the tree is a basket [or bowl] of tree agate stones [or beads]. This stone will hold the energy of today's ritual and connect it to the Tree of Life so that you can work with it later. When you feel ready, walk up to the tree and take your gift from the basket."

When everyone has received an agate, arrange everyone into three concentric circles around the tree with crones and sages in the middle ring (assuming you have enough people, otherwise have everyone in one circle). Instruct the group that the middle ring is to go widdershins while the other two rings are to go deosil as you chant (if you have only one ring, go deosil). Lead the group in the chant "Standing Like a Tree" for as long as the chant wants to go.

Serve the cakes and ale and let people eat and relax for about five minutes. When everyone is fin-ished and ready to move on, have the elemental priest/esses dismiss the quarters starting in the North:

"We thank you, Auriel, Archangel of the Northern realms, for you have held us steadfast and guarded our rite. Go if you must, stay if you will. Hail and farewell.

"We thank you, Gabriel, Archangel of the Western realms, for you have awakened us and guarded our rite. Go if you must, stay if you will. Hail and farewell.

"We thank you, Michael, Archangel of the Southern realms, for you have transformed us and guarded our rite. Go if you must, stay if you will. Hail and farewell.

"We thank you, Raphael, Archangel of the Eastern realms, for you have inspired us and guarded our rite. Go if you must, stay if you will. Hail and farewell."

At the end of each dismissal the priest/esses draw the banishing pentacle for that element. Open the circle in the same way that it was cast. Say, "Merry meet, merry part, and merry meet again" or whatever ending is traditional for your group to indicate that the ritual is over. ❧

Exploring Sensuality

WHERE: Outside or Inside

CAST: HP/S, a skilled drummer or two

MINIMUM NUMBER OF PARTICIPANTS: Two

RITUAL DRESS: Your choice, something comfortable

PROPS: Tiny bottles of lotion or massage oil (travel size), some unscented, and a basket to put them in while you hand them out to the group

ALTAR SETUP: One main altar with the necessities and images of Hathor and Pan (or deities of your choice)

CAKES AND ALE: Grapes, crackers, cheese, sparkling apple cider

NOTES: A *menat* is a special crescent-shaped necklace with beaded strands worn almost exclusively by Hathor, and was shaken during ritual to honor her. If there are any disabled people in your group, such as the blind or the deaf, go ahead and give the meditation as written, but allow them some time during the ritual to describe how they experience the sensual world if they want to do this.

Perform basic housekeeping such as announcements and so on.

Cast the circle as desired, perhaps using a fragrant incense like rose or amber, and scented water or diluted rose water. Call to the four directions/watchtowers as desired. Now call to the Goddess and God (you can substitute deities if you like):

"O Hathor, Golden One, daughter of Ra, blue-lidded Lady of the dawn, red-lipped dancer of the Gods, come to us, bring us your perfume, your gentle touch, the music of your *menat* and sistrum, your movement and dance. We honor you as you honor us. Welcome and Blessings, Lady.

"O Pan, Lord of the wood, great satyr, goat-foot God, dancer in the green, come to us, bring us your sense of humor, let us run our fingers through your fur and smell your warm fragrance, let us hear the sweet music of your pipes as we dance with you. We honor you as you honor us. Welcome and Blessings, Lord."

Ask everyone to be seated, then give the meditation:

"Relax, close your eyes, and take a deep breath. Let it out, and take in another deep breath, feeling the air enter your lungs. Let it out and feel that sensation as well. In and out . . . keep breathing slowly and deeply, feeling the air entering you and leaving you. You can also feel the ground [or floor if you're inside] underneath you, and other things around you like the temperature of this place.

"You can also hear things. (*Describe the sounds of the place—floor creaking if you're inside, birds and bugs if you're outside, etc.*) You can also smell things. Don't move, but take a moment to fully explore your surroundings with only touch, hearing, and smell. (*pause*)

"We are spirits in physical bodies, and so we experience reality as a physical thing, as a series of things that touch our senses. We touch, we taste, we hear, we smell, we see. And anything else we can pick up with our sixth sense is welcome, too, of course.

"Speaking of seeing, slowly open your eyes and look around. See the people across from you, and all around you. Look around the circle, and this space that we occupy. Notice everything that you can, perfect and flawed. Combine what you see with what you hear, feel,

and smell. Take a moment to fully experience this place . . . open your senses wide and drink. (*pause*)

"Now take a couple more deep breaths and stand up. (*Cue the drummer(s) to get ready.*) Let us come back inside our bodies so that we can use them as tools to express ourselves. One of the most sensual and primal ways we can express ourselves is through body movement, so we will simply be swaying and gently moving to the drumbeat. Close your eyes if you like so that you can fully listen to the drum(s) and interpret what you hear and feel without distraction."

Cue the drummers to begin a slow and steady beat. It can be a complicated beat, but you don't want people dancing all over or flailing their arms and crashing into their neighbors, so keep it slow. You just want swaying and some sinuous arm movements. Continue the beat without speeding up for a couple of minutes, then gently and gradually taper it off. When the drumming is over, move on to the next section:

"Take a deep breath and open your eyes. How does your body feel? (*pause*) Now, everyone turn to your left so that you're facing your neighbor's back. Reach out and touch their shoulders, and gently give them a shoulder and neck rub. Everyone should be both giving and receiving. Can you imagine a world without touch?

"As you give, notice what the other person's shoulders and neck feel like. As you receive, notice what the other person's hands feel like and how they move on your skin. If you like, you can send a bit of gentle healing energy along so that it circulates around to everyone. *(Pause; let them go for a couple of minutes.)*

"Stop when you're ready, and thank the person behind you."

Give out the cakes and ale, enlisting help from people as needed, saying:

"As you enjoy this, take your time and eat slowly. See the food and drink, enjoy its aroma, taste it on your tongue, observe its texture, its color, how it feels in your hand and mouth. . . . Savor this bounty of the Earth. Appreciate it. Fully experience every molecule."

Give people a few minutes to experience their food and drink, then give out the lotion, letting people choose which one they want:

"This basket contains scented and unscented lotion [massage oil] for you to use at home. Use it to explore the sensual world as you rub it into your skin or someone else's skin. Again, take your time as you feel it on your skin, experience its aroma if it has a fragrance, look at its color and texture, but please don't taste it."

When everyone has chosen a lotion bottle, close the ritual by first thanking the Goddess and God:

"Hathor, Lady of the sensual world, we give praise unto you and thank you for your help with this ritual. We thank you for helping us to explore the senses of these bodies. Praise to Hathor! Blessings and farewell.

"Pan, Lord of the dance, we give praise unto you and thank you for your help with this ritual. We thank you for helping us to explore the senses of these bodies. Praise to Pan! Blessings and farewell."

Dismiss the elements/watchtowers and open the circle in the same way that these were done at the beginning. Say, "Merry meet, merry part, and merry meet again" or whatever ending is traditional for your group to indicate that the ritual is over.

Medicine Wheel

WHERE: Outside

CAST: HP/S

MINIMUM NUMBER OF PARTICIPANTS: One

RITUAL DRESS: Comfortable clothing

SUGGESTED SONGS: "I Circle Around" (traditional Ghost Dance song), "Firedance" and "Thunderbird" by Peter Buffett

PROPS: Matches, white sage bundle, abalone shell, sweetgrass braid, rattle (or small bone whistle, or clapper stick, other traditional instrument for your area), pitcher of water, tobacco (or cornmeal, acorn flour, cattail pollen, other traditional offering materials for your area), drum

ALTAR SETUP: One small central stone altar to hold supplies (see above) surrounded by a wide circle of stones, with larger stones marking the cardinal directions.

CAKES AND ALE: Cold water

NOTES: Make *sure* you know which direction is which—there will be no color cues to help you once the ritual has begun. If necessary, place a flower or leaf on the Eastern stone to help you remember which direction to face. If

you choose not to have recorded music for this ritual, at least bring a drum and, if possible, get a group of several drummers to help out for the Ghost Dance.

Perform basic housekeeping such as announcements and so on. Light the white sage bundle and consecrate the circle by walking around it clockwise. Give a blessing prayer to the land and sacred space:

"Blessings to you spirits of the land, bones of Mother Earth, ancestors, ancient ones. We honor you today and ask your permission that we may honor you and the Great Spirit in this place, in this circle of sacred space. We honor the great hoop of the world today in this place. We honor the two-leggeds, the four-leggeds, the no-leggeds, the swimmers, and the winged ones today in this place. May we walk the sacred path today in this place. May it be so."

Now use the sage bundle to bless the tools that will be used for the ceremony, and finally bless each person in turn. Take up the rattle and stand facing the East, shaking the rattle loudly for a few seconds. Pour out a small libation of water and a pinch of tobacco. Say:

> "Spirits of the East, where the sun rises, place of the morning star, spirits of the winged ones of the winds, we call upon you now. Awaken, fly to us, bring us your blessings and wisdom. Hear our prayers."

Moving to the South, again use the rattle, offer water and tobacco, and say:

> "Spirits of the South, place of innocence and youth, place of learning, spirits of deer, mouse, coyote, and mountain lion, we call upon you now. Awaken, come to us, bring us your blessings and wisdom. Hear our prayers."

Moving to the West, use the rattle, give the offerings, and say:

> "Spirits of the West, place of the setting sun, place of healing and introspection, spirits of the swimmers, bear, and insects, we call upon you now. Awaken, come to us, bring us your blessings and wisdom. Hear our prayers."

Moving to the North, use the rattle, give the offerings, and say:

> "Spirits of the North, place of rest, place of wisdom, place of winter and death, spirits of buffalo, grizzly, those who live underground, we call upon you now. Awaken, come to us, bring us your blessings and wisdom. Hear our prayers."

Replace the sage, water, and tobacco and turn to the other participants, saying:

> "The medicine wheel is a lifelong path to walk. The circle is sacred to all people, and represents the wheel of the year, the cycles of the seasons, and the life of a being. The things we do here today, and the way that we do them, honor this place, honor ourselves, honor our ancestors, and honor all our relations. The Medicine Wheel has its name because it heals . . . heals us as we travel and learn, heals the land through blessings and energy, and heals the world as we work connected with other shamans in other places as one great spiderweb.

> "First, we will work to heal ourselves today, because if we are not whole and pure and sacred, we will have a hard time bringing that wholeness and sacredness from the wheel out into the rest of the world. We will also work for protection today . . . protection for the magic-workers that we may continue to heal the world, and protection for the earth against those who would greedily rape her. For without the earth, we have nothing.

> "Let us learn from the earth and her creatures now. We will walk around the wheel four times as we sing a sacred Ghost Dance song that many Pagans today know. After the fourth round I will stop where I began, but you need to keep walking until you reach the point in the wheel that you feel most drawn to. Then we will sit down

and listen to what the earth and her spirits wish to tell us."

Begin to sing "I Circle Around" and when about half the people have picked up the chant, start walking rhythmically and slowly around the medicine wheel in a clockwise direction. Go around four times, and stop where you started as you finish the fourth time around. When everyone has found where they need to be in the wheel, stop the song and sit down. Now say:

"We will still ourselves, close our eyes, and just listen for a time. Listen to what the earth wants to tell you."

After about five minutes, quietly say:

"If you are in deep meditation, you need to begin your return journey. You'll have another minute to come back."

After one more minute, quietly say:

"It is time for our second working. Come back to yourself . . . breathe deeply . . . and when you are ready, open your eyes and be here now."

Have everyone take a couple more deep breaths and stretch a bit, then let them know what will be happening for the protection working:

"For this part, we will be dancing for protection. The Ghost Dance took place to try to pro-tect the native people from the whites who were taking their lands and killing them. There are now people of other spirit paths who wish us destroyed, and people who would like to see the earth destroyed to feed their wallets. May we honor the ancestors of this place and all our relations as we ask the Great Spirit for protection from hostility and greed.

"So dance now! Dance with your power animal if you have one, dance the message that the earth gave to you! Become invisible to harm like a ghost, and give energy to the earth for her protection. This is a holy dance, a sacred dance . . . let yourself be one with the Great Spirit."

Play *Firedance/Thunderbird* if you have a CD player set up, or begin drumming a fast dance rhythm. Keep drumming until people seem to have gone into trance and are coming back out again—use your judgment so that people have long enough to do their working but not so long that they are overly exhausted, especially if the day is hot.

When the dance is over, invite people to sit down and quickly give them water. After a minute or two, encourage people to share their visions with the group if they like. When all have rested and shared their stories, stand and get the rattle, water, and tobacco from the central stone. Use the rattle for a few seconds, then pour out some water and a pinch of tobacco as an offering to the Great Spirit. Then say:

"Great Spirit, Mother Earth, ancestors, all our relations, we honor you. We give you our lives as you give life to us. We give you gifts as you give to us the gifts of visions, power, and love. May we never forget this. May we honor you every day, in everything that we do. Thank you for coming to us and blessing us. Thank you for blessing this place and making it sacred. Thank you for helping us work magic. Be with us always."

Say, "Merry meet, merry part, and merry meet again" or whatever ending is traditional for your group to indicate that the ritual is over.

Candlelight Labyrinth Procession

WHERE: Outside or inside, at night

CAST: HP/S, four element priest/esses

MINIMUM NUMBER OF PARTICIPANTS: Five

RITUAL DRESS: Black for the HP/S, black or element colors for the four priest/esses

SUGGESTED SONGS: "The Circle Is Cast" by Robert Gass, "Now I Walk in Beauty" (traditional Native American), "She Changes Everything She Touches" by Starhawk or "We Are an Old People" by Morning Feather and Will Shepardson

PROPS: Tape or flour and diagram to make the labyrinth (or pre-made canvas labyrinth), CD player, feather fan and/or incense, tiki torch and holder (such as a bucket of sand), glass chalice full of water, large cluster of crystals or large open amethyst geode, small table or wooden TV tray, white taper candle in holder, small white taper candles and paper bobeches or little paper cups to catch wax drips, large cauldron that can hold water, food dye, assortment of tumbled gemstones, soft towels or cloths for people to dry their hands on if desired (bring extras in case one gets dropped into the cauldron water)

ALTAR SETUP: One large altar with the necessities, small table at the labyrinth entrance to hold lit white taper in holder plus paper bobeches or cups and small white tapers

CAKES AND ALE: Your choice

NOTES: Arrive at the ritual site far in advance to lay out the labyrinth pattern, which can be based on a historic design or designed by you (but the design must have an entrance and exit—don't use a design that only has a one-way path to the center or you'll have an instant traffic jam). Indoors, use masking tape to lay out the labyrinth, outdoors use flour powder or small stones. Allow plenty of room for people to walk and pass by each other undisturbed, from about thirty inches to thirty-six inches is a good width for the labyrinth paths. There are some websites on the internet that show how to lay out a labyrinth if you need help.

Also in advance, be sure to have everyone practice the circle casting procession so that you have each person's entry and circuit timed with the music and no one is left standing around waiting for her part to begin. Do a dress rehearsal in the actual ritual space if possible so everyone knows when they need to be halfway around, and so on.

Before everyone arrives, place the cauldron in the center of the labyrinth. Fill the cauldron with water to a depth of about six inches and pour the assorted gemstones into it for people to take out when they reach the center. Add a few drops of food color to darken the water if the stones are visible (don't add too much or people will end up with dyed hands). Neatly fold and lay the towel on the edge of the cauldron for people to use if they like.

Perform basic housekeeping such as announcements and so on.

Call up the four element priest/esses and have the Earth priest/ess pick up the crystals. Start the song "The Circle Is Cast" and have the Earth priest/ess begin slowly walking around the outside of the labyrinth area, holding up the crystals or geode for all to see. At the halfway point in that verse, he or she should be at the halfway point around the circle. When the first verse ends, he or she should be back at the main altar and the next priest/ess should be ready to begin walking on "By the air . . ." If the previous person isn't back yet, that's okay—have him or her continue to walk around the circle back to the altar. The second priest/ess lines up to the right of the first.

Continue until Water has returned to the main altar and lines up behind Fire. At this point, all four priest/esses begin processing around the circle as before but all together in a line, one behind the other. This continues until the song is over. If you prefer, have the priest/esses leave their objects on the main altar and dance around the circle faster and faster as the music builds, or even have everyone get up and begin circling around with the priest/esses until the song is over if the mood is right.

Now give everyone a description and introduction to the history and purpose of the labyrinth:

"Before we walk the labyrinth, I'd like to tell you a bit about the origins of this truly ancient symbol and how it has been used.

"The labyrinth can be historically traced from ancient Greece and Crete, with some examples dated to about 1200 BCE, but labyrinths are also found throughout the world, including Scandinavia, India, Europe, and the Americas.

"Unlike the maze, which has many false paths and dead ends to fool the visitor, a labyrinth has one true path that leads to the center. Over time and depending on the culture various things have been found at the center, but most frequently the labyrinth has been used to represent the seeker's path to spiritual enlightenment.

"Walking the labyrinth teaches us to slow down, to contemplate the path rather than the goal. If we walk the meandering path with purpose, rather than rushing to the goal directly, we find that we begin to reflect on ourselves and our own path.

"According to some sources, medieval labyrinths in churches were used to replicate long pilgrimages to sacred sites. Perhaps you could use your trip inside this labyrinth for this purpose. Perhaps you could reflect on your current position on your sacred path. Perhaps you could view it as the seeker's path from start to finish in its entirety. However you choose to use your time inside the labyrinth, remember that it is an ancient, rare magic that should be savored.

"Let us sing together as we wait to enter, and you can also sing as you walk if you like. Light your candle as you enter . . . let it both light your way and represent your spirit on the path to the center of all. At the center, you will find the cauldron of death and rebirth . . . reach in and find what Spirit has to offer you. Let it represent what you need to further your way along the path . . . when you have finished at the center, find the path out. You may blow or pinch out your candle once you have left the labyrinth.

If you are inside, dim the lights (but not to pitch black, allow enough light for people to see the path). Lead everyone in the song/chant "Now I Walk in Beauty" at a slow tempo as you stand behind the small wooden table and light the taper. As each person reaches you, place a bobeche on a small white taper and give it to them, indicating that they are to light it from the larger taper and enter the labyrinth.

Obviously, it will take some time for everyone to slowly walk the labyrinth. Allow as much time as it takes for this section, even if you are running overtime (you can cut out the "change" chant if need be). When the last person has exited, serve the cakes and ale (you could pour a libation into the cauldron as a nice touch if you wish). When everyone has enjoyed their food and drink, lead them in the chant "She Changes Everything She Touches" or "We Are an Old People."

Now the elemental priest/esses thank the elements and open the circle at the same time, beginning with Water. Have him or her take the chalice and walk widdershins around the circle, saying:

"Teachers, spirits, guardians, and powers of Water, we thank you for your gifts to us tonight. You are forever blessed and honored. By the power of Water, the circle is open."

Repeat for the other directions, each priest/ess taking up their element's symbol, walking widdershins around the circle, and saying:

"Teachers, spirits, guardians, and powers of Fire, we thank you for your gifts to us tonight. You are forever blessed and honored. By the power of Fire, the circle is open.

"Teachers, spirits, guardians, and powers of Air, we thank you for your gifts to us tonight. You are forever blessed and honored. By the power of Air, the circle is open.

"Teachers, spirits, guardians, and powers of Earth, we thank you for your gifts to us tonight. You are forever blessed and honored. By the power of Earth, the circle is open."

Say, "Merry meet, merry part, and merry meet again" or whatever ending is traditional for your group to indicate that the ritual is over.

Exploring Dance and Movement

WHERE: Outside or inside (inside is probably better for people with bare feet)

CAST: HP/S, several good drummers

MINIMUM NUMBER OF PARTICIPANTS: One

RITUAL DRESS: Your choice

ALTAR SETUP: One main altar with the necessities, if desired

CAKES AND ALE: Hearty bread and apple juice

Perform basic housekeeping such as announcements and so on.

Briefly introduce the ritual and how it will be done:

> "Welcome. Today we celebrate movement of the body as a source of magic. We will be creating sacred space with movement, raising energy through dance, and communing with Spirit through moving meditation.
>
> "Even if your movements are restricted and you are unable to get up and dance with abandon, please try to participate as best you can in your own way. The idea is not to be professional ballerinas—we're exploring how to use our physical bodies to induce trance and make magic. Now, let's get started by casting the circle and calling the elements with movement only."

Begin casting the circle. As you move around the space, make whatever motions you feel are appropriate to create the sacred space, whether that means dancing, walking while using arm movements, crawling, whatever. Do the same for the four elements, using intuitive motions to call Air, Fire, Water, and Earth. Encourage everyone to work with you.

When that's been completed and you're satisfied that the circle has been cast and the elements are present, ask everyone to be seated and give the history of dance and movement related to ritual in history:

> "Dance and ritual movement are one of the most basic human behaviors known. Even small infants will instinctively bounce to songs with a clear rhythm, and children will soak up new songs and dance to them even more willingly than they will eat their dinner. We have all been moved to sway or clap to certain songs or ritual moments, even unconsciously.
>
> "As far back as recorded history allows, we find images of dancers. From Africa to Europe, Asia to America, dance both for pleasure and ritual has been an integral part of every culture. Even today, we can see movement and dance as an important part of every entertainment in modern society and as part of achieving an altered state of consciousness during ritual.
>
> "The Quakers and Shakers got their names from the involuntary trembling of their bodies during religious services; the Appalachian snake-handling sects of Christianity use rhythmic dance and movement to entrance themselves; many African-American congregations use both music and movement to celebrate the Holy Spirit; Native American medicine people and shamans of other cultures use movement and dance to work with their power animals, move to other planes of existence, and otherwise achieve trance; African dance is both used in its traditional form in Africa as well as part of the descendant religions of Santería [*san-ter-ee-ah*], Voudou, Candomblé [*can-dom-blay*], and so

on; and then of course there's the Witches and Pagans of today who use the spiral dance and many other forms of music and movement to raise energy.

"Now let's all get up and move. Even if you can't stand, move with us as best you can. Shake out your arms, shake out your legs, stretch, and take a deep breath. *(Cue drummers to start slowly and quietly.)* We'll be raising energy through free dance, so do whatever feels good—this ain't a beauty pagent. Raise that energy and send it where it needs to go; it's your energy so it's your choice where to send it. Let's go for it!"

Cue the drummers to get a little faster and louder and begin dancing, encouraging everyone else to join in. If they're skilled and experienced drummers, they'll know how long to drum and when to end the session—if not, you'll need to cue them when the energy peaks and tell them when to stop. Make sure you know whether or not they can handle the job alone before the ritual begins!

When the free dance is over, ground your energy and make sure everyone else does the same so you don't have anybody floating away on you. Have everyone be seated so you can give the meditation:

"That was great! It's a fine example of letting yourself simply be in your own headspace, while at the same time working with others to raise energy and avoid crashing into each other too much. Free movement, simply doing as the Spirit tells you without questioning the result, is one of the purest forms of expression.

"Now take a deep breath, relax, and close your eyes. Concentrate on your breathing as you relax, letting your heart rate slow down . . . letting your breathing slow down . . . let your body rest now. Without moving, think about movement. Think about how dance has affected your life. *(pause)*

"What kind of dance do you like to watch? What kind of dance do you like to do? How are they different? *(pause)*

"Think now about the kinds of dance that there are in the world. You've heard of many kinds . . . free dance without form . . . the elaborate choreography of a music group or a movie . . . belly dancers . . . African tribal dance . . . Native American dancing at pow-wows . . . Celtic dance, which gave birth to square dancing and cloggers . . . *(pause)*

"Martha Graham was an American modern dancer of the twentieth century who broke convention and stripped dance down to its basic elements of movement. She also studied the works of religious scholars and philosophers, with many of her choreographies bearing such names as 'Heretic,' 'Primitive Mysteries,' 'The Gospel of Eve,' and 'The Song of Songs.'

"Graham described a dancer as an athlete of God, whose practice is an act of vision, of faith, in which the dancer cultivates grace in the form of a heightened sensitivity to the miracle of the human body. *(pause)*

"It is in this search for the connection from our physical world to the world of Spirit that we dance. It is the link between our bodies and the other planes of existence. Between our souls and the soul of the Great Spirit.

"Breathe deeply and prepare to dance once again. Move your body a little bit at a time until you're ready to open your eyes. Prepare yourself to enter the paradox of using your body to leave your body. When you are ready, be here now. *(Pause while people open their eyes and stretch.)*

"You are probably familiar with the term *whirling dervish*, even if you're unfamiliar with who or what it means exactly. *Dervish* literally means 'doorway,' because these special Muslim practitioners become doorways for Allah as they spin around and around in trance. This ancient tradition, dating back to the thirteenth century, is part of serious religious ritual, and is not one we will attempt to reproduce exactly, for many reasons. But since we have already danced the path of chaos, it would balance things to dance the path of order as the dervishes do.

"Spread out, giving yourself plenty of room between you and your neighbors. If at any time you feel you must stop spinning, please try to get yourself out of the way of others and sit down. If you feel you must slow down, that's fine too. Remember, we're not tornadoes, nor are we experienced Muslim dervishes. Do what you can so you can get a taste of this type of movement in ritual. Let's begin."

Again, cue the drummers to begin slowly at first, and begin spinning in place slowly. As the drummers speed up, you will need to stop and check on the other participants, helping and reminding people as necessary to avoid accidents. Let the dance continue for about five minutes, then cue the drummers (if necessary) when it's time to stop.

Ground yourself, leading by example, and make sure everyone else does, too. Dissipate any extra energy, then move on to the bread and juice. When everyone has rested and enjoyed the food, dismiss the elements and open the circle, again using movement only to do this and enlisting everyone's help. Say, "Merry meet, merry part, and merry meet again" or whatever ending is traditional for your group to indicate that the ritual is over.

Honoring Creativity

WHERE: Inside unless art materials can be used outdoors

CAST: HP/S

MINIMUM NUMBER OF PARTICIPANTS: One

RITUAL DRESS: Your choice

SUGGESTED SONGS: "She Changes Everything She Touches" by Starhawk

PROPS: Art supplies, such as paper and drawing supplies; collage boards, magazines, and glue; clay; mask forms, glue, feathers, and sparkly stuff; and so on. Use whatever you think people would enjoy working with in the time allotted and with the size of group you will have—the larger the group, the easier to work with and less messy the materials need to be.

ALTAR SETUP: One large central altar with room for all the necessities

CAKES AND ALE: Your choice

NOTES: Have everyone bring drums and rattles, and have extras on hand for those who didn't bring any.

Perform basic housekeeping such as announcements and so on.

Use your creativity to invent a new way to cast the circle and call the elements. You could ask everyone to help you in his or her own way, or use only different sounds, or paint an instant intuitive picture on the spot and hang it in the appropriate direction, and so on. Get creative!

Now invoke deities of the arts:

"We call to Ptah [*tah* or *pet-ah* . . . either is correct], the divine craftsman . . . we call to Brigid, muse of metals . . . we call to Lugh [*lew*], master of all the arts . . . we call to Arachne [*ah-rack-nee*], weaver supreme . . . we call to Khnum on whose potter's wheel humans were created . . . we call to Minerva, the wise goddess of a thousand works . . . we call to you, oh Ancient Ones of creativity, of a thousand peoples, of a thousand lands, of a thousand years . . . help us touch you as you touch us . . . help us to create! Welcome, and blessings to thee."

Lead everyone in the chant "She Changes Everything She Touches," having the men sing "He" instead of "She" to add balance and honor the male gods of creativity. Either continue the chant as people are making their projects, or end the chant as you see fit. Before they begin their projects, a brief explanation is in order (if they will be chanting while creating, give this before starting the chant):

"Creation is not only the work of the Gods: we can create wonderful things as well. We can draw upon Spirit to guide our minds and our hands, and in turn, we can give our creations back in honor of Spirit. We can charge them with purpose . . . we can make and then ritually destroy them . . . we can keep them on our altars . . . we can use them in spellwork or prayers . . . what you make, how you make it, and what you do with it is up to you. Today we will be using these supplies to make [type of thing] and charging them. Let's get started! Get comfortable, let your creativity flow free, guided by Spirit, and have a good time with it."

Hand out the supplies or, if the group is not too large and there's enough room, let them come up and pick out just what they want. Allow plenty of time for people to create what they need. When most people are done, give a five-minute warning for people to finish up (there are always a few who take a very long time to make anything, so they may need to be prodded a bit).

If the materials are messy, like clay or paint, be sure to provide baby wipes or another way that they can clean off their hands when they're done.

Also provide a place to store projects if they need time to dry, and/or plastic bags to put projects in to get them safely home if need be.

When time is up, let them know, then move on to charging the items with energy. You can either state a purpose for everyone's project, such as unity or something reflecting the season, or let each person decide toward what to direct the energy. To charge the items, have each person hold his or her own item as the group intones a single note together. You will want to start the note and keep it going until you sense that enough energy has been raised and directed.

Now have people set aside their projects and pick up their instruments for some creativity drumming. Introduce this section by saying:

"Creativity is not just physical arts and crafts. Creativity includes all the arts, such as music. Let's have a good old-fashioned drum jam so you can exercise your musical and rhythmic crafting, too! Everyone put away your projects, grab your drums and shakers, and let's make some music. If you don't have a shaker, I have extras up here, or you can simply clap, or dance, or sing, or whatever you like to add your creative spark to the group."

Give people a moment to collect their instruments, then lead or have someone lead the group with a strong and simple drumbeat. Let the beat get more complicated as the group really gets going, but be careful not to let it degenerate into chaotic noise! The drumming should peter out on its own eventually, or you can bring it to a close if the ritual is running long by using drumming signals or a high voice trill.

After the drumming, move directly into the cakes and ale to refresh everyone. Allow a few minutes for everyone to eat and drink, then prepare to close the ritual. First, thank the deities you called to join you:

> "Hail and praise to you, Old Ones of the arts, creativity's muse . . . Ptah the craftsman, Brigid the bright arrow, Lugh of the spear, Arachne the weaver, Khnum the potter of life, Minerva the maker . . . we can never thank you enough for coming to us, your children, your creations . . . may you love us as we love you and honor you through our creative works. Go if you must, but stay in our lives to inspire us if you will. Blessed Be."

Dismiss the elements and open the circle in the same ways that these were done at the beginning of the ritual. Say, "Merry meet, merry part, and merry meet again" or whatever ending is traditional for your group to indicate that the ritual is over. ❧

SUGGESTED READING AND LISTENING

Books

Amberston, Celu (Cornwoman), *Deepening the Power: Community and Sacred Theatre*. Victoria, BC: Beach Holme Publishing Ltd., 1995.

Blood, Peter, *Rise Up Singing: The Group Singing Songbook*. Bethlehem, Penn.: Sing Out Publications, 1988.

Bonewits, Isaac, *Rites of Worship: A Neopagan Approach*. Miami, Fla.: Dubsar House Publishing, 2003.

Clifton, Chas S., *Modern Rites of Passage* (Witchcraft Today series, book two). St. Paul, Minn.: Llewellyn Publications, 1994.

Cunningham, Scott, *The Complete Book of Incense, Oils and Brews*. St. Paul, Minn.: Llewellyn Publications, 1989.

Ellis, Normandi, *Awakening Osiris: The Egyptian Book of the Dead*. Grand Rapids, Mich.: Phanes Press, 1988.

Foster, John L., *Love Songs of the New Kingdom*. New York, N.Y.: Charles Scribner's Sons, 1974.

Hugin the Bard, *A Bard's Book of Pagan Songs*. St. Paul, Minn.: Llewellyn Publications, 1998.

Lichtheim, Miriam, *Ancient Egyptian Literature*. Vol. II, The New Kingdom. Berkeley, Cal.: University of California Press, 1976.

Madden, Kristin, *Pagan Parenting: Spiritual, Magical & Emotional Development of the Child*. St. Paul, Minn.: Llewellyn Publications, 2000.

Marks, Kate, ed., *Circle of Song*. Lenox, Mass.: Full Circle Press, 1994.

Middleton, Julie Forest, ed., *Songs for Earthlings*. Philadelphia, Penn.: Emerald Earth Publishing, 1998.

Monaghan, Patricia, *The New Book of Goddesses and Heroines*. St. Paul, Minn.: Llewellyn Publications, 1997.

Starhawk, M. Macha NightMare, et al., *The Pagan Book of Living and Dying*. New York, N.Y.: HarperCollins, 1997.

Stein, Diane, ed., *The Goddess Celebrates: An Anthology of Women's Rituals*. Freedom, Cal.: The Crossing Press, 1991.

Telesco, Patricia, *The Wiccan Book of Ceremonies and Rituals*. New York, N.Y.: Citadel Press, 1999.

Music

Alan, Todd & Friends, *Carry Me Home*. CD. Fire Seed Publishing, 1992.

Buffett, Peter, *Spirit: A Journey in Dance, Drums and Song*. CD. Hollywood Records, 1999.

The Chieftains, *The Chieftains 8*. CD Claddagh Records Limited, 1978.

Elfman, Danny, *The Nightmare Before Christmas, Original Motion Picture Soundtrack*. CD. Disney, 1993.

Galway, James, and the Chieftains, *In Ireland*. CD. RCA/Ariola International, 1987.

Gaia's Voice, *Chorus of Life*. Cassette. Self-produced, 1990.

Hamouris, Deborah and Rick and Friends, *Welcome to Annwfn*. CD. Bigsky Studios, 2001.

Libana, *A Circle Is Cast*. CD. Spinning, 1986.

McKennitt, Loreena, *The Visit*. CD. Quinlan Road Limited, 1992.

———, *To Drive the Cold Winter Away*. CD. Quinlan Road Limited, 1987.

Mediaeval Baebes, *Undrentide*. CD. Nettwerk America, 2000.

Murphy, Charlie, et al., *Canticles of Light*. CD. Serpentine Music, 1997.

Ó Dhomhnaill, Mícheál, and Paddy Glackin, "Sweeney's Buttermilk." *Celtic Christmas IV*. Windham Hill Records, 1998.

On Wings of Song and Robert Gass, *Ancient Mother*. CD. Spring Hill Music, 1993.

Radcliffe, Jessica, et al. *Beautiful Darkness*. CD. High Bohemia Records, 2000.

Reclaiming and Friends, *Let It Begin Now*. CD. Reclaiming Records, 2001.

Sansone, Maggie, *Traditions*. CD. Maggie's Music, 1989.

Silver, Elaine, *Faerie Goddess*. CD. Silver Stream Music, 1997

Siva, Sri, *Dancing with Siva Mantra Music*. CD. Vaaak Sounds, 2002

Sweet Honey in the Rock, *Breaths*. CD. Flying Fish Records, 1992

Vangelis, *Heaven and Hell*. CD. Windham Hill Records, 1997.

XTC, *Apple Venus*, vol. 1. CD. Idea Records Ltd., 1999.

———, *Skylarking*. CD. Caroline, 2002 (remastered version).

INDEX

ABOUT THE AUTHOR

 illow Polson, Pagan for most of her life, describes her current path as an eclectic blend of Kemetic, Wiccan, and whatever the land itself whispers on the wind. The author of *Witch Crafts, Sabbat Entertaining,* and *The Veil's Edge*, Willow is active in Pagan rights and the growing Pagan clergy community. She lives in Stanislaus National Forrest, California, overlooking Yosemite National Park. Please visit her Web site, www.willowsplace.com.